REFLECTIONS
REFRACTIONS

Alexis Dirks
Annie MacDonell
Sheree Hovsepian
Sanaz Mazinani
Aura Satz
Brea Souders

REFLECTIONS REFRACTIONS

black dog publishing
london uk

CONTENTS

INTRODUCTION

Reflections & Refractions has come together as a way of marking Gallery 44's 35th anniversary. Founded in 1979 by a small group of artists for the purpose of sharing a darkroom and studio space, G44 has expanded to support award-winning education and exhibition programming and production facilities for nearly 350 members. As a way to mark the occasion, this publication is meant as a non-linear reading into some of the topics explored by the gallery's ever-evolving programming.

The format of this publication is significant. As an artist-run centre, G44 is practiced at taking risks, at fostering programmatic adaptability and in realizing projects that privilege experiment and dialogue. The publication is divided into three sections, in which each section brings together two artists whose work shares a common thread. In order to emphasize the conversational tone of much of our programming, each chapter features eight short essays by a wide range of international contributors, including artists, curators and writers. The contributors were selected by G44 and the artists and were invited to offer an object/image response. While each contributor is specifically responding to a single artwork or project, no parameters were set for the tone or approach. While some tend towards the essayistic, others are decidedly poetic and experimental. Again, this format, which concurrently invites a focusing-in and a more fluid and alternative means to engage photo-related discourses is a reflection of G44's openness to different approaches to criticality.

Anniversaries tend to peddle in nostalgia, but also seem to enable reflection on that pivotal space between what has happened and where we might find ourselves after the occasion has been marked. In other words, anniversaries encourage a simultaneous looking forward and backwards. With this in mind, we have put together a group of artists who have been part of our history or are slated for future collaboration and a group of writers that includes both active contributors to G44 and new collaborators. But perhaps more significantly for this context, anniversaries encourage an allowance for self-reflexivity. In thinking about the past 35 years we have turned our attention inwards, and started to look more closely at the relationship between our spaces of exhibition-making—the gallery—and art-making—the facilities, which include darkrooms and a digital lab. As such, the axis along which the artists featured in this publication meet is around the theme of interiors. *Reflections & Refractions* takes us inside of the apparatus, as is the case with Aura Satz's *Doorway for Natalie Kalmus*, 2013, and *Oramics: Atlantis Anew*, 2011; into the sites of production as with Sheree Hovsepian and Brea Souders's studio assemblages; into the prism of image construction as with Sanaz Mazinani; and we are led deeper into the archive (or library) by Annie MacDonell and Alexis Dirks.

In Chapter I, Aura Satz (London) and Sanaz Mazinani (Toronto, San Francisco) are brought together as both artists share a tendency towards a self-consciousness around the apparatus, whether the physical apparatus or the apparatuses of seeing, display and perception. Aura Satz engages with, amongst other things, women's impact on cinematic technology. In *Oramics: Atlantis Anew*, 2011, Satz introduces Daphne Oram's aptly named Oramics Machine through meditative images of the device's inner workings. A central figure in the development of British experimental electronic music, Oram was also the cofounder of the BBC Radiophonic Workshop in 1958. The film reanimates this technological relic, emphasizing the visual nature of Oram's pioneering drawn sound principles used to compose electronic music. Natalie Kalmus is another important reference for Satz. In the film *Doorway for Natalie Kalmus*, 2013, she sojourns inside the lamphouse of a 35mm colour film printer, exploring its technicolor prismatic and kaleidoscopic effects. Natalie Kalmus was the ex-wife of Herbert Kalmus, the cofounder and president of the Technicolor Motion Picture Corporation. She was the colour consultant on hundreds of films, including *The Wizard of Oz*, 1935, and was part of a workforce of women whose treatises for colour use in film, advertising and fashion defined new standards for the employment of and engagement with colour.

The prism and kaleidoscope also feature in Sanaz Mazinani's practice. In her digital collage works Mazinani juxtaposes found images from the Internet: for example, American soldiers carrying a flag-draped coffin, taken from the US Department of Defense website, with an image from Facebook of a young man, dressed in army fatigues, posing for a self-portrait (*Redacted March #3,* 2013). Her photographic montages use images relating to the destabilizing effects of war in order to disrupt reductive notions of the original image as merely a reflection of reality. Through repetition and reproducibility media images are unsettled, shifting the ways in which conflict is visualized. In other works Mazinani offers a critical reassessment of the ideological and ontological mechanisms of photography and invites a closer reading into how images are constructed. *Landscape #27*, 2011, for instance, shows the variation between the same image being taken by flipping through the white balance settings of a camera. This exploration into the comparative qualities of light was one of the first images taken by Mazinani when she first moved to California, and provided an important inquiry into the differences in light between the west coast and Toronto. The device appears in the work of both Satz and Mazinani as itself and as an invitation to consider the complexities of image production and consumption.

The studio becomes the focus of Chapter II with artists Sheree Hovsepian (New York) and Brea Souders (New York). For both Hovsepian and Souders the studio and the darkroom are sites of experiment while also spaces for exploring the discursive possibilities of object-ness, movement and abstraction. Sheree Hovsepian's photographic works evolve from an ongoing series of photograms—photos made without a camera by placing objects directly on photographic paper—called *Haptic Wonders*, 2012–13. The term "haptic" means relating to or based on the sense of touch. This reference to touch refers to Hovsepian's production of these works in the darkroom and her directing various materials within a very specific moment in time. The photograms, therefore, are not simply the result of a precisely timed and delicate process but are also a performative recording of the artist's body as she physically manipulates and repositions objects on the light-sensitive surface. Hovsepian's *Haptic Wonders* are then paired with multi-media, wall-based installations called *Material Gestures* and bronze and wood sculptures that develop as a tangent to the photograms by emulating their forms.

Brea Souders also haptically takes up the materials of the studio. After a decade of shooting, Souders was left with a generous archive of unusable compositions, failed experiments and products of mechanical errors. In an attempt to clean up this refuse she began cutting up the film and sorting it into plastic sleeves for disposal. Souders noticed that static electricity would hold the small pieces in place, which led her to explore this process more formally in *Film Electric*, 2012. She scatters the cut-up pieces of film over larger pieces of acetate that are rubbed against a hard surface to activate static cling. In a kind of disorderly emergence, some fragments cling together while others are repelled and fall to the ground. The large sheets that retain this momentary sculpture are then hung on a wall and photographed. In an analogous project, *Mountains Without Faces*, 2013, Souders gathers the fragments into neatly composed geometric forms, allowing the shards to re-form into a compositional whole. While there is a precisely tuned visual language at work here, Hovsepian and Souders are open to the possibility of accident and uncertainty, allowing intuition to assist in their ongoing negotiations with static and light.

Finally, Chapter III emphasizes process with Annie MacDonell (Toronto) and Alexis Dirks (Yellowknife). Alexis Dirks culls found images and assembles these into three-dimensional sculptures along with other appropriated objects—architectural debris, rocks, core samples, and so on. Rather than allowing the images to adapt to their new positionality as sculptures, Dirks re-flattens the images by photographing her tableaux. As with images such as *Folded Statue,* 2014, there is a successive incursion into dimensionality as the photograph of a statue is restaged as a three-dimensional object which is then returned to the two-dimensional plane of the photographic image. Dirks's material pairings often reach across the past and present, while conflating, as she notes, geological and human histories. Made clear by her image *Keystone*, 2012, Dirks borrows from various sources and time periods, compelling a more malleable archive.

Annie MacDonell's similarly appropriative approach offers a critical entry into discourses of representation, authenticity and authorship. In her project *Pictures Become Objects, Objects Become Events*, 2014, MacDonell mined images from the Toronto Public Library's Picture Collection to produce several works, including a progressing mural and vitrines installation, a performance and a book. MacDonell is interested in how these images, collected by the library's many female librarians, over many years, have the potential, when reframed through this ongoing project, to become an idiosyncratic feminist archive. In her 2013 work, *Flatness, Light, Black & White*, MacDonell introduces a series of digital collages taken over the course of an afternoon at a local barbershop. The interior details of the barbershop are available through glimpses of mirrors, doorways, and various accouterments. As MacDonell notes, the images are not simply documentary but offer an entry into the formal qualities of the photograph in the digital age—through images that are inclined towards mutability, compression, and an ever-expansive visual field. In many ways, MacDonell and Dirks share an interest in repositioning and recontextualizing images within the slippery space between linearity and spatial disjuncture and between image and object.

This is by no means an exhaustive survey of the complex and nuanced practices of the six artists presented in the publication. It is simply meant to offer a glimpse into some of the highlights featured in the pages that follow. There are many other relationships that could easily be made between all of the artists and by that token many more points of departure. But these are notes for another publication, for another time. Ultimately, each artist negotiates various physical or dialogic interiors, making us acutely aware of the mechanisms of image production and circulation.

We hope you enjoy the many perspectives offered here and we hope these introductions encourage you to think more broadly and deeply about contemporary photography. We would also like to thank all the artists and contributors for making this publication possible. We are most grateful for their wisdom, keen investigatory skills and for encouraging new ways of looking.

Noa Bronstein
Managing Editor, Executive Director, Gallery 44

PRODUCTION

Aura Satz and
Sanaz Mazinani
Genevieve Yue
Kate MacKay
Esther Leslie
Peggy Gale
Caoimhe Morgan-Feir
Gabrielle Moser
Benjamin Sutton

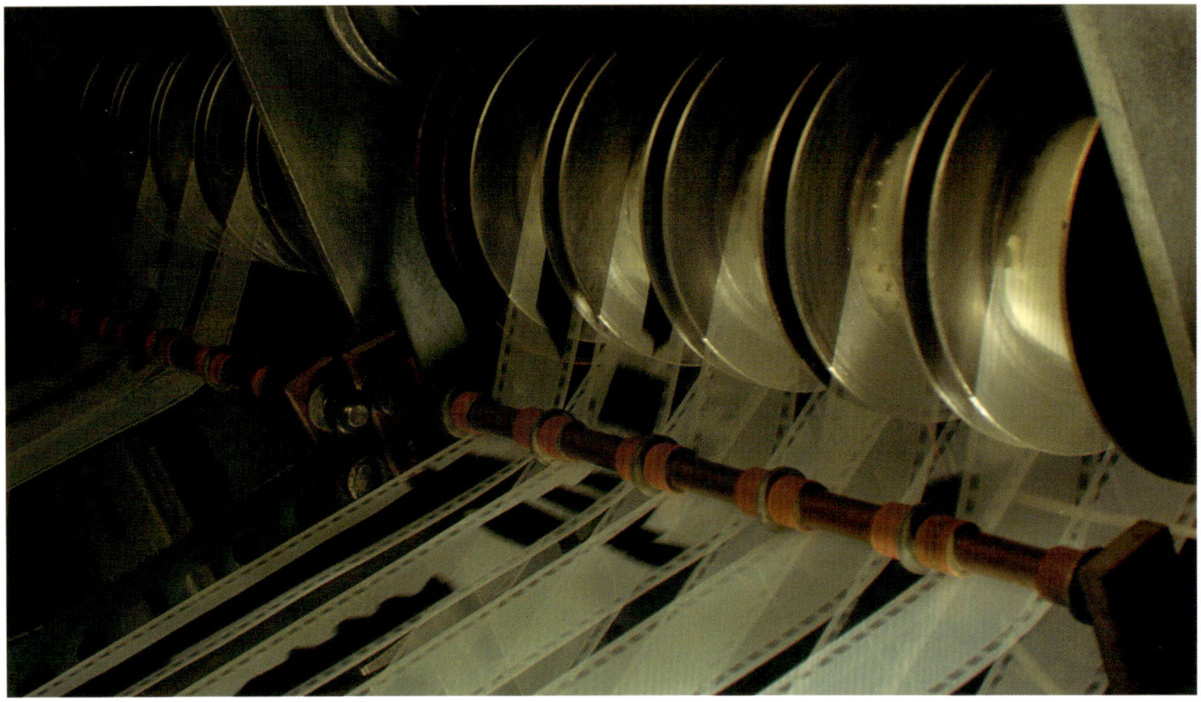

Aura Satz, *Oramics: Atlantis Anew*, 2011 (still)
Courtesy of the artist

The Oramics Machine, a 1959 synthesizer built by electronic music pioneer Daphne Oram, was lost for many years. In 2009 it was rediscovered in a French barn. The machine, a large metal rack and a smaller wooden chest painted white, was transported back to England, where it currently resides behind a glass case at the Science Museum in London. It is too fragile to function in its current state, though Oram left behind many wondrous, otherworldly recordings created with her instrument.

Aura Satz's *Oramics: Atlantis Anew* matches these recordings, along with Oram's voiceover musings on the interrelations between sound, music, and human existence, to her camera views of the machine. Though the Oramics Machine is in many ways cinematic—it is a device that reads passing filmstrips for aural, rather than visual information—Satz constructs sound and image relationships that are more imaginary. With each plunk of Oram's score, Satz's camera shifts perspective. Her close-ups study the intricacies of the machine: a small numeric counter, and various pieces of tape labelling a knob "A double-flat" or, more forebodingly, a lever marked "do not use".

With *Oramics*, we see the (re)animating capabilities of cinema. Satz plays the role of conjurer, adding movement, sound, shadow and light to a musical instrument that, absent of its creator, does not work. She films the Oramics Machine not as a dusty, cobwebbed relic, but as an intricate organism imbued with its own vitality. Aided by Oram's ethereal compositions, the film conveys something on the order of the uncanny: a ghost in the machine.

This more spiritual aspect of the film, an element common to Satz's practice, is also manifest in Oram's own work. Oram was the founder of the BBC Radiophonic Workshop in 1958, which produced electronic sounds for television and radio, and she was keenly interested in the potentially curative effects sound could have on individuals, particularly at a mass scale. In *Oramics* we hear her read aloud from sections of her 1972 book *An Individual Note: of Music, Sound and Electronics*. Human beings, she argues, contain "tremendous chords of wave patterns 'sounding out the notes'". Existence, then, is a matter of harmonics. Additionally, part of the film's title comes from "Atlantis Anew", a 1960 manifesto written by Oram in which she theorizes the healing properties of sound: A person's disturbed "innate waveform" might be restored with a soundhouse and its corrective harmonics.

If sound has the potential to restore balance to those who "have fallen out of sorts", it follows that one must have the ability to modify and modulate it. The Oramics Machine, correspondingly, not only produces sounds through graphic models, but alters their pitch, vibrato, reverberation and envelope shapes. A sonic healing machine, furthermore, must be immersive. The individual not only listens to the sound, but her body should be placed in direct contact with its tones and vibrations. Though the component pieces of the Oramics Machine do not amount to an enclosed soundhouse, Satz's film places the viewer-listener deep within the machine and makes virtual the experience.

At the end of the film, a hand appears for the first time to lower the lid on the white chest housing the Oramics Machine's waveform scanners. This is also the film's first wide shot, and in actual scale the device seems smaller than the rest of the film has imagined it to be. We already know, however, the potency of the treasures within. Here is a vessel that might contain the secrets of the lost civilization of Atlantis, sounds to align humankind with the universe, "summation tones penetrating the very fundamentals of these worlds beyond our frontiers."

Genevieve Yue

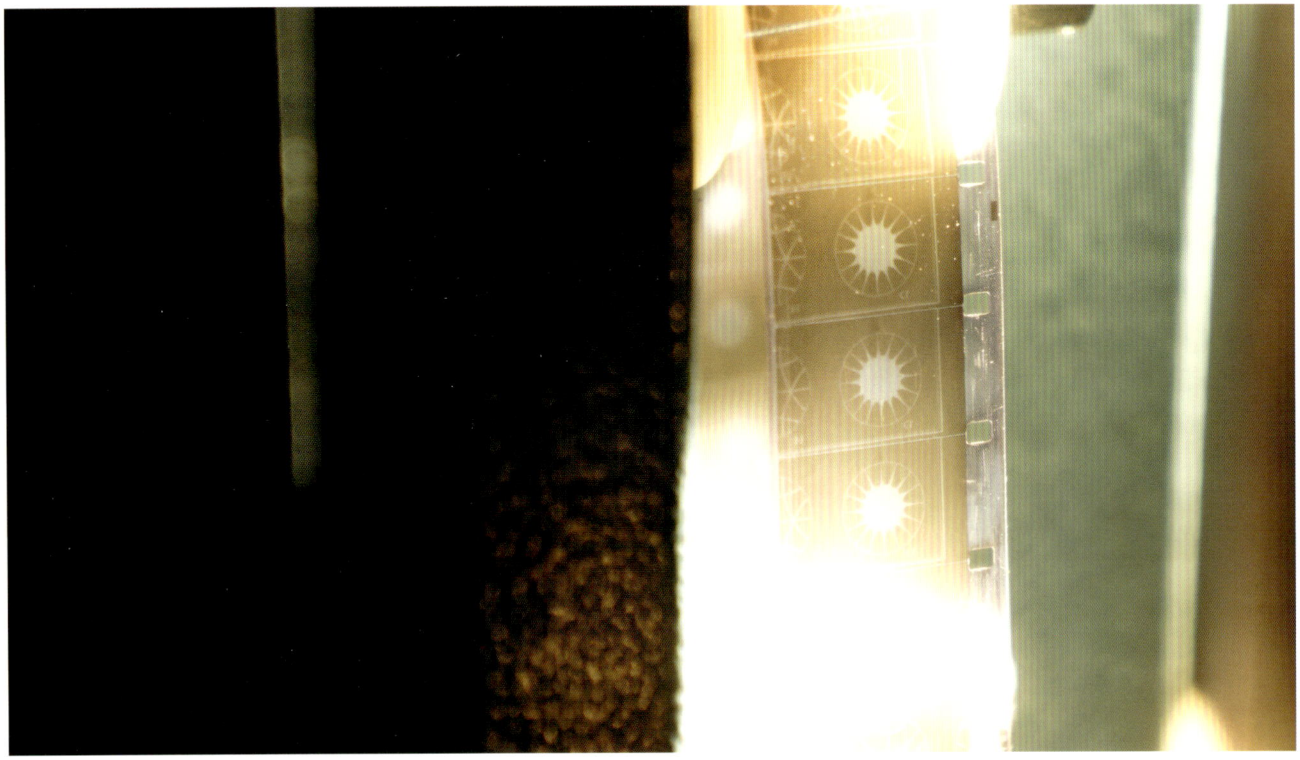

Aura Satz, *Universal Language: A Lost Manifesto*, 2012 (still from 16mm film)
Courtesy of the artist

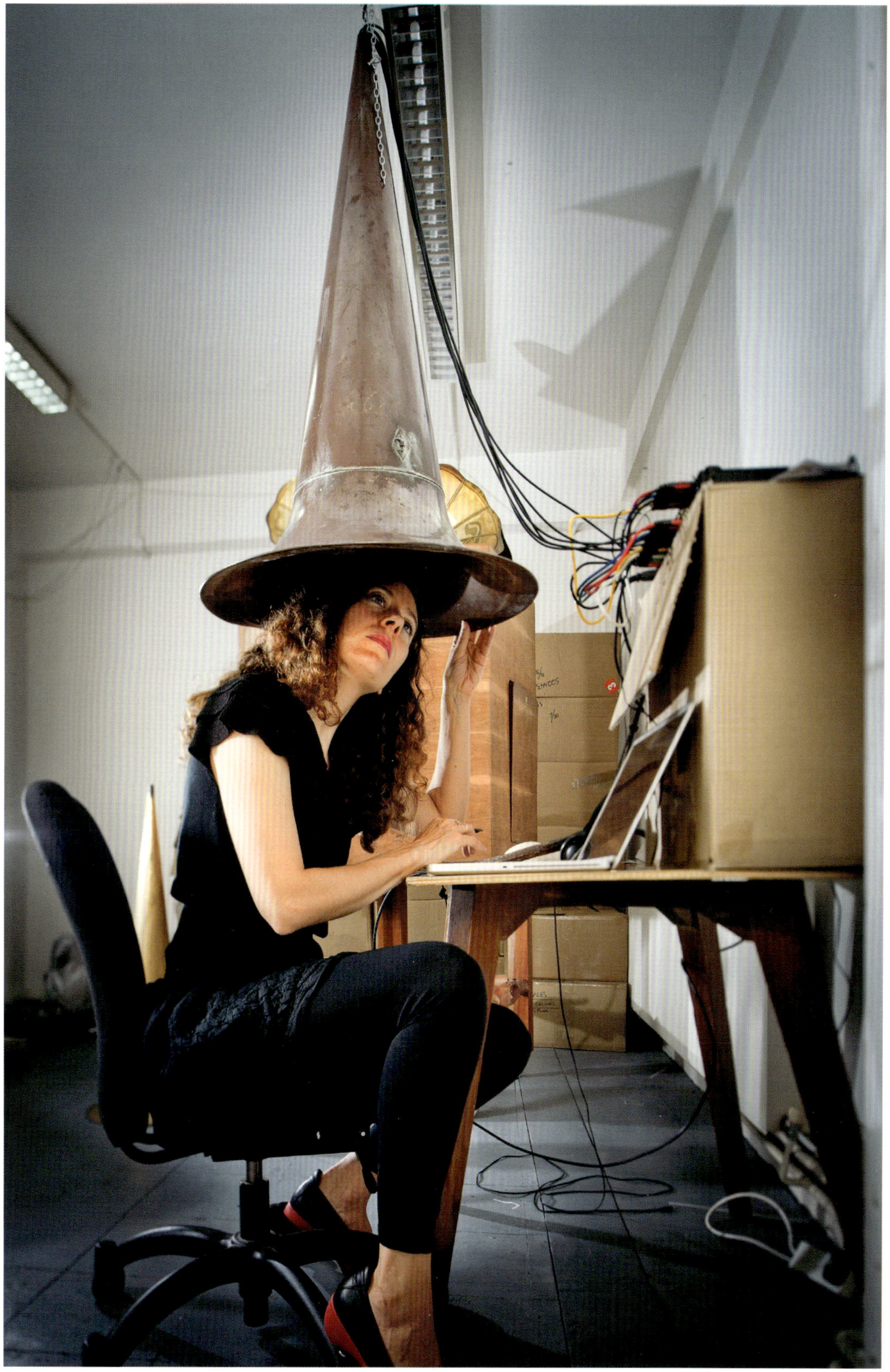

Aura Satz, *Spiral Sound Coil* (in the studio), 2010
Photograph by Paul Winch-Furness
Courtesy of the artist

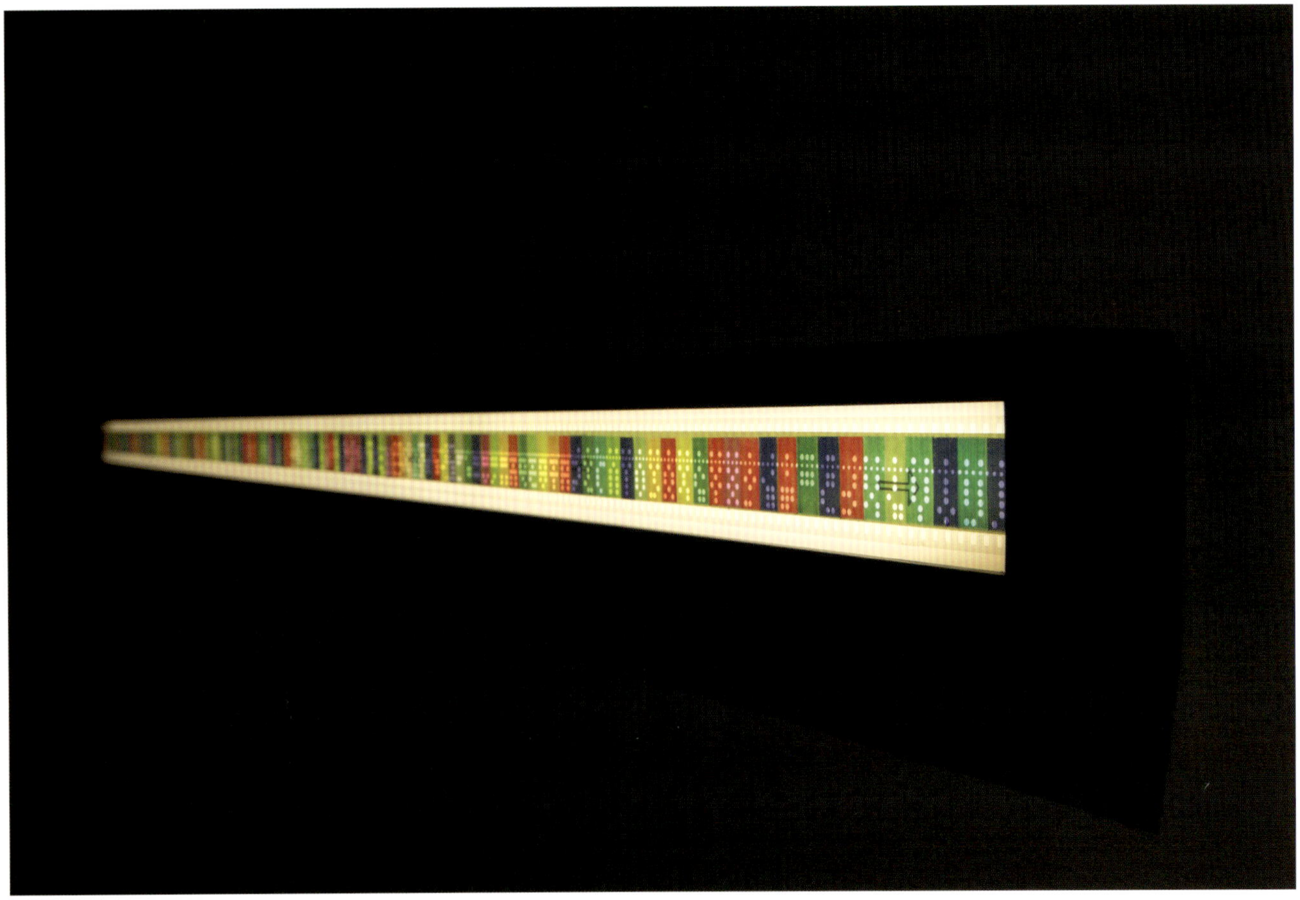

Aura Satz, *Colour Score*, 2013
58 x 3 inch filmstrip, ink and perforated paper,
lightbox, Gallery 44 Centre for Contemporary
Photography, Toronto
Photograph by Morris Lum

From the wax cylinder to the Chladni Plate; from optical soundtracks for films to flaming Rubens's tubes; from the frequency hopping technique, patented by movie star Hedy Lamarr and composer George Antheil: to early cinema colour processes; Aura Satz's works explore the resonances of analogue technologies and experiments for the recording and transmission of sound and image. Delving into the ways sound and image are scored, coded and translated—and mindful of the social context and the conditions of labour that create and are used to apply these tools—Satz's films, performances and installations provide a layered and subtle look at nineteenth and twentieth century invention.

Functioning both as a compliment to and a key for understanding her video *Doorway for Natalie Kalmus*, 2013, Satz's colour-code works also evoke the rich history in the development and use of colour in the cinema. Kalmus was the wife of and collaborator with inventor Herbert Kalmus, who early in the twentieth century developed the Technicolor process for printing moving images in colour. The patented process was one of the first methods to allow colour to be added to film mechanically, and was continuously refined and employed throughout the last century. Natalie, who had a background in fine art history, was assigned the responsibility of assuring that colour be employed to its best advantage by the studios and her name appears in the credits of almost all Technicolor productions from 1933 and into the 1950s. *Doorway* allows us access to the colour-bathed interior of the Colour Grading machine, or more specifically, the Bell & Howell lamphouse. While developed later than the time period in which Kalmus was working, this interior presents the same palette that Kalmus would have used as she worked to develop a coherent colour score for each film.

Satz's 35mm colour code works serve as physical notations for the colours that we see in the projection they accompany. These abstract colour works are inspired, not only by Kalmus, but also by the 16mm film work of Paul Sharits and the late nineteenth-century colour organs of Alexander Wallace Rimington. Rimington sought to create a new art form by freeing colour from its attachment or service to objects to allow it to be appreciated in a pure form. His device enabled him to project colours in sequence by pressing particular keys on the machine, enabling him to create a kind of visual music made of pure colour. Satz's 35mm *Colour Score*, 2013, consists of a punched paper strip that dictates the mechanical rhythms and colour in *Doorway for Natalie Kalmus*. The punch holes determine to what degree each valve should be opened to adjust the RGB balance and subsequently the colour of the film. On the gallery wall the framed strip has a mysterious quality, like a fragment of a lost language or hieroglyph. Similarly, her 35mm *Film Strip*, 2013, provides a sculptural embodiment of the colours we see in the film and the order in which they appear. Like Sharits's *Frozen Film Frame*, 1971–76, panels that pack 16mm films in plexiglass, Satz's twist of polyester film stock represents a moment of time stopped while also serving as an ode to the beauty of a medium that is becoming increasingly rare.

Kate MacKay

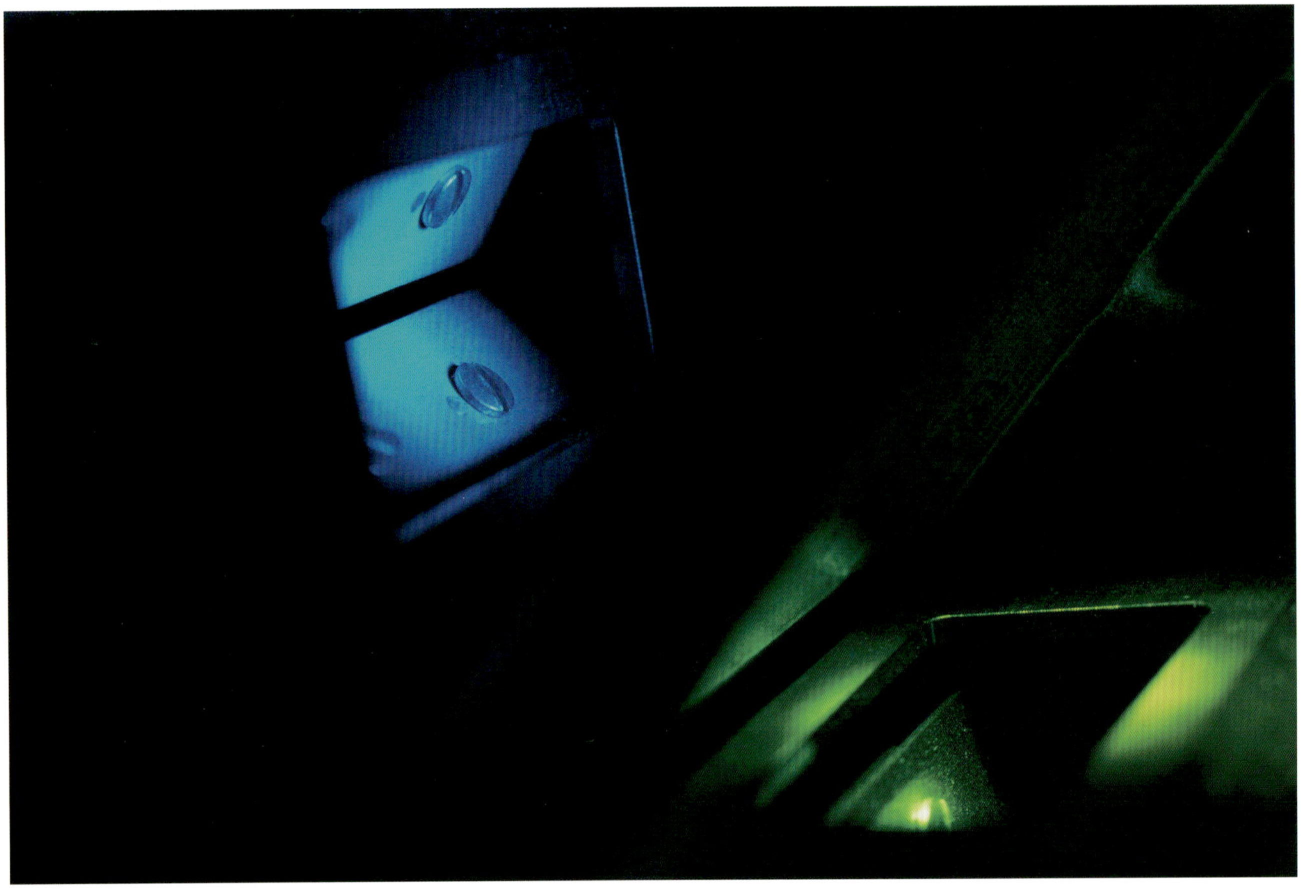

Aura Satz, *Doorway for Natalie Kalmus*
2013 (still)
Courtesy of the artist

Colour is both real and fantastic. Colour is just a coating or it is the body of the thing itself in all its hues. These polar views of colour as dreamlike and as lifelike have been flung around by chromophobics and chromophiliacs alike and annexed to questions of taste, kitsch, artfulness, quality, 'primitivism', and sophistication.[1] Colour in film, known best in its commercial-industrial guise as Technicolor™, was excoriated by critics in its early days. Colour appears to be too visible, a malevolent, autonomous actor disturbing the story on screen. But Technicolor was not banished from the movies. It clung to the screen, while the cities blazed everywhere with new synthetic colours, and colour appeared to have become a compulsion.[2]

If it could not be banished, then it needed to be tamed. Natalie Kalmus, an important reference in Satz's work, battled in her role as Technicolor colour advisor to rein in colour's perceived excesses and to establish the proper, tasteful use of colour. A controversial figure who, by all accounts, seeded conflict everywhere, she drafted colour rules that held sway for some years. Her manifesto text *Color Consciousness*, 1935, argued that the advent of colour was the last stage in film's ability to "duplicate faithfully all the auditory and visual sensations" in an "enhanced Realism".[3] But duplicating reality is inadequate. Film is the artform of the twentieth century and must deploy colour not as a documentary record but as a part of its creative translation of the world.

Kalmus countered the extent to which colour, vector of fantasy, appeared to be a matter for scientists and not part of the craft of filmmaking. Colour needed aesthetic rules, adhered to by colour artists, and viewers needed to develop a "colour sense".[4] Kalmus recommended the following rules in order to downplay the oppositionality inherent in colour: the use of excessively bright or saturated colours should be avoided in favour of more harmonious, 'natural' and less intense colour schemes; warmer and brighter shades should emphasize only important information pertaining to the narrative—otherwise neutrals should be used. Kalmus's conception of colour emphasized harmony—wrought from the antagonism that is colour. The reference was musical and the film was to be scored for colour. Thereby it evoked a long-standing association of musical scales and colour scales, as well as numerous experiments in relaying between musical tones, emotional tones and visual tones.

Colour is brought into view by Satz in *Doorway for Natalie Kalmus*, a film that explores the prismatic effects of the lamphouse of a 35mm Technicolor film printer. Humans and machines are often conceived as oppositions, but colour streams between them. The sounds of the mechanism in *Doorway* emphasize the annexing of human and machine, their yoking and their opposition. Here, the senses are flooded with pure and intense colour, with colour direct from its source in the machine, colour without alleviation, colour broken free of narrative. The "colour sense" demands not a sensibility, but an adequate organ of the body-mind that might go up against it. In *Doorway*, the colour spills out from the screen. It bathes us for as long as it hangs around. It kisses the eye and skin and flies on. It puddles on the ground and evaporates. It is an ungraspable substance of desire and our lust is annexed to the machinery that produces and destroys it.

Esther Leslie

1. For some of these perspectives, see David Batchelor, *Chromophobia*, London: Reaktion, 2000, an exploration of the various ways in which colour is perceived as dangerous or trivial or both and "other to the higher values of Western culture". See also Michael Taussig, *What Colour is the Sacred?*, Chicago: University of Chicago Press, 2010, on colour's association with the "primitive".
2. See Blaszczyk, Regina Lee, *The Color Revolution*, Cambridge, MA: The MIT Press, 2012, p 191.
3. Kalmus, Natalie, "Color Consciousness", *Journal of The Society of Motion Picture Engineers*, no 2, August 1935, p 140.
4. Kalmus, "Color Consciousness", p 140.

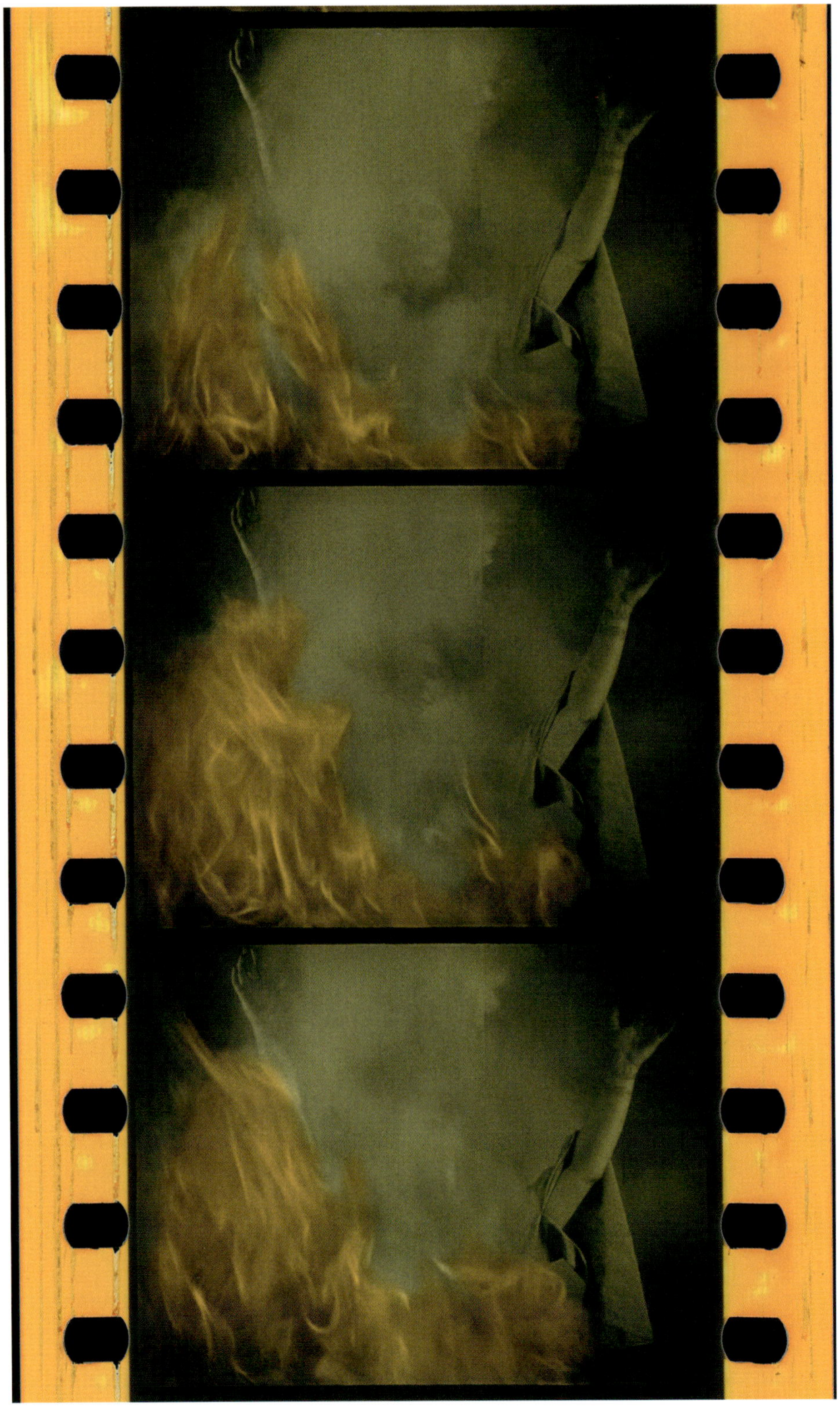

Aura Satz, *Joan the Woman–with Voice #2,* 2013
18 x 28 x 8 inch duratrans print framed in lightbox with audio
Courtesy of the artist

Colour blares from the screen and it elicits reactions. It has done so from the very beginning. Films from the 1890s, some of the first film strips that exist, are paeans to the glories of colour: swirling skeins of vibrantly coloured, ever-changing chiffon are twisted by girls performing butterfly and serpentine dances. These virtually abstract films accounted for around one third of films made in the first 20 years of cinema. All of the 'fathers' of cinema made this type of film: Thomas Edison, William Kennedy Dickson, Louis Lumière and Paul Nadar. The colours were applied to each film frame by hand.

Colour's workings on the eye are the result of work, first by the hand and then by machines too. In 1980, the filmmaker and theorist Peter Wollen, in the grip of Structuralist film phrases, observed that there is no direct link between the colour of the natural world and the colour of the projected colour film. Indeed, "a whole technology of dyeing has intervened".[1] Moments in the history of technologies of dyeing are indicated in Aura Satz's series *Colour Opponent Process*, 2013. For one, there is the orange cloud of fire laid on by semi-mechanized stenciling in *Joan the Woman—With Voice*, 2013, a series of three photographic lightboxes showing the final moments of Cecil B deMille's 1916 silent feature. Here is an inaugurating event in a history of colouring technologies that couple human labour to machinic labour. As emblematic of this, *Joan the Woman* slips into the background, into the medium itself, its colour obscuring and blotting out, while a buzz of noises chatters around her.

Technology has its technologists, which means large workforces of colour makers, fixers, appliers, wipers, developers, correctors and so on. The colourful world of dreamy confection is predicated on the dull, grey world of labouring for colour, labouring to make colour, process it, capture it, distribute it, classify it. Colour work has often had a female dimension. There was Kalmus, of course. But there have been other women who found a leading role in the production or organization of colour. Mary Hallock Greenewalt with her mobile colour machineries for theatre and cinemas was one, for which she received 11 patents between 1920 and 1934, including one for a portable light and music phonograph for the home.[2] Greenwalt insisted that to each feeling there corresponds a colour and she called her art of playing with these "Nourathar". These were amongst the "high priestesses" of colour.[3] But not the least part of female colour work was in the factories where colour was processed for film and photography. At Pathé's and Gaumont's factories in the 1910s and 1920s, hundreds of women used pantographs and needles to make stencils for film prints, which could then be coloured en masse. Colour produced by labour, a labouring that permanently stains the hands and insists its minions work in near-darkness, is received by its audiences as the antithesis of what made it. It comes to audiences as evanescent light. It is transient and transcendental.

In Satz's work colour appears always as something else. It stands in opposition to itself. Colour is liquid. Colour is light. Colour moves. Colour covers. Colour highlights. Colour gives shape. Colour is made by machinery and chemicals. Colour is made in the eye. Colour is consumable. Colour is work. Colour cultivates. Colour wipes out. Aura Satz lets us stand in its doorway, its portal to somewhere else, to itself.

Esther Leslie

1. Wollen, Peter, "Cinema and Technology: A Historical Overview", in Teresa de Lauretis and Stephen Heath, eds, *The Cinematic Apparatus*, New York: St. Martin's Press, 1980, p 24.
2. There is plentiful material on Greenewalt's life and work on the website of The Historical Society of Pennsylvania. http://hsp.org/sites/default/files/legacy_files/migrated/findingaid0867greenewalt.pdf, accessed January 10, 2014.
3. "High Priestess" was screenwriter Arthur Laurents's sarcastic name for Kalmus, in his account of her conflicts with Alfred Hitchcock when working on *Rope*. See Laurents, Arthur, *Original Story By, A Memoir of Broadway and Hollywood*, New York: Alfred A Knopf, 2000, p 134.

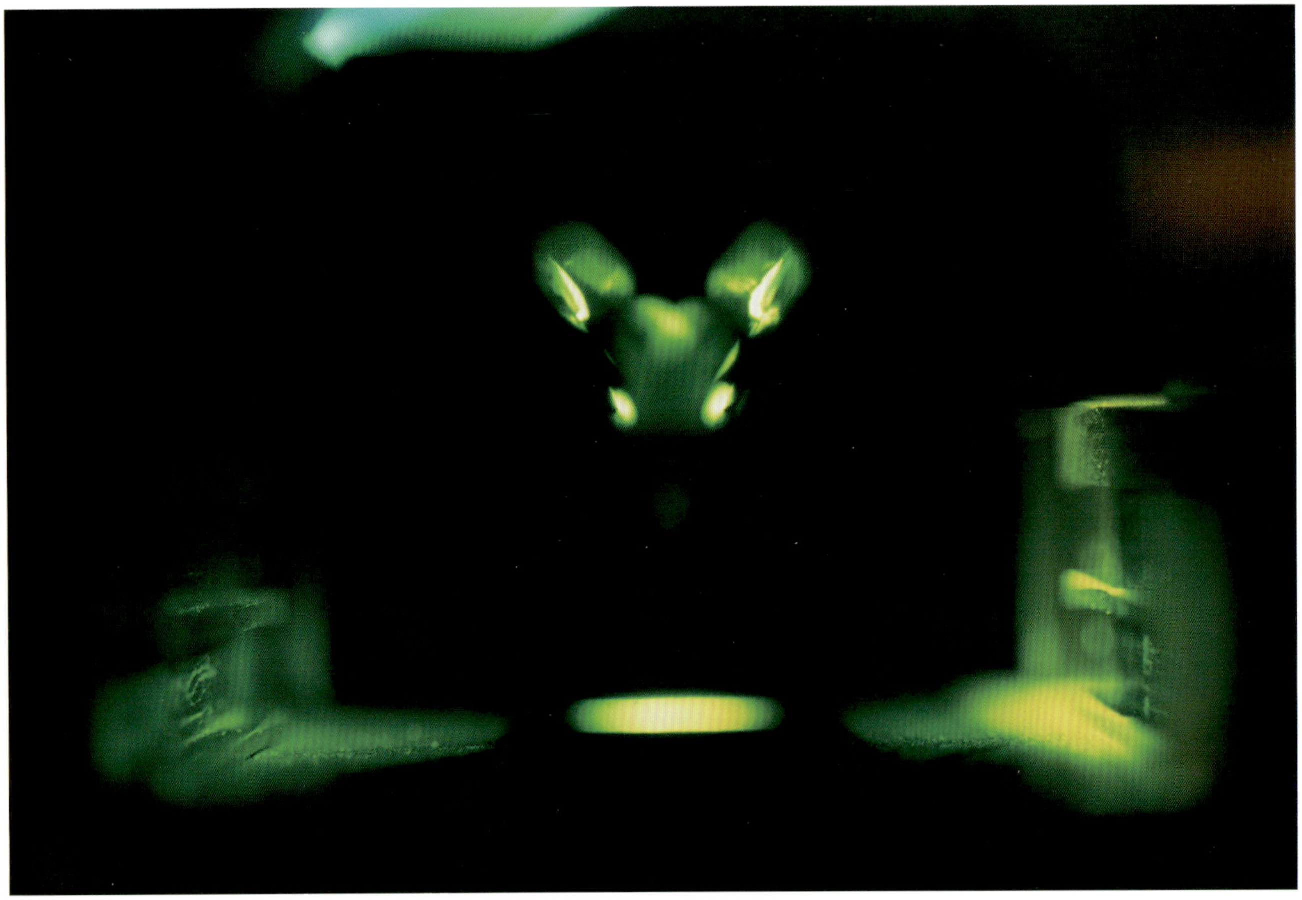

Aura Satz, *Doorway for Natalie Kalmus*,
2013 (still)
Courtesy of the artist

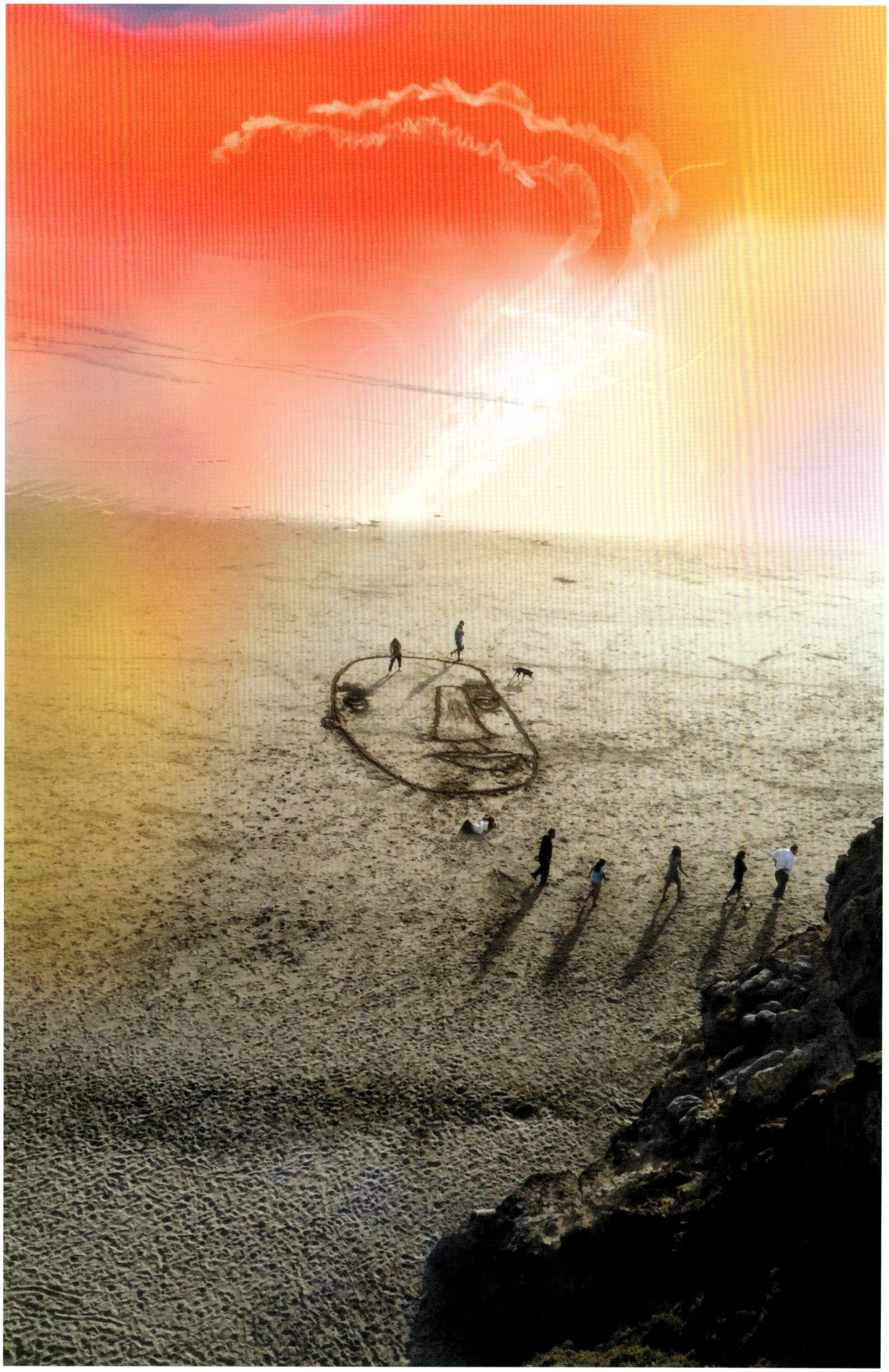

Sanaz Mazinani, *Ground Portrait*, 2010
6 x 9 inch pigment print
Courtesy of the artist and Stephen Bulger Gallery

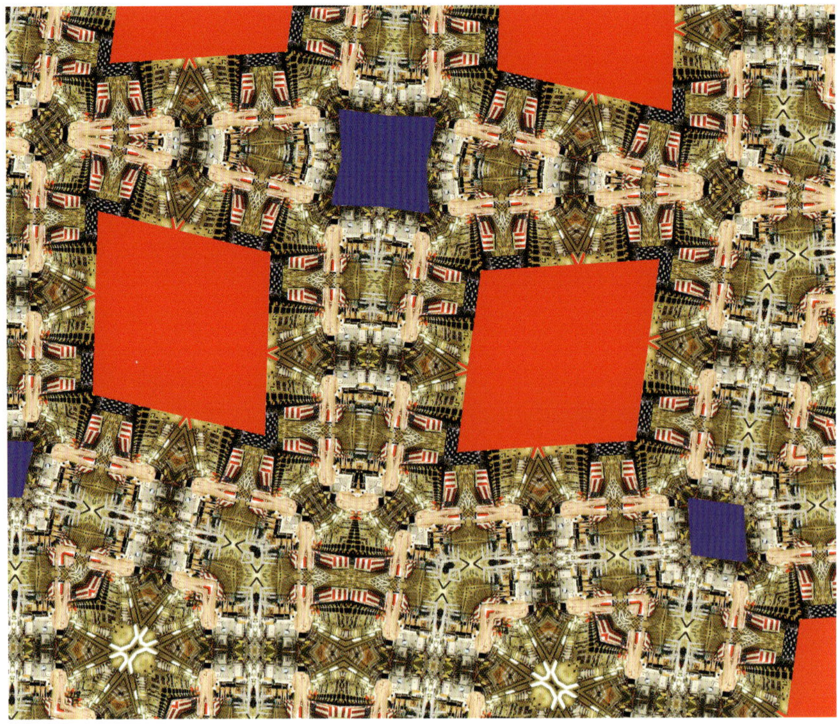

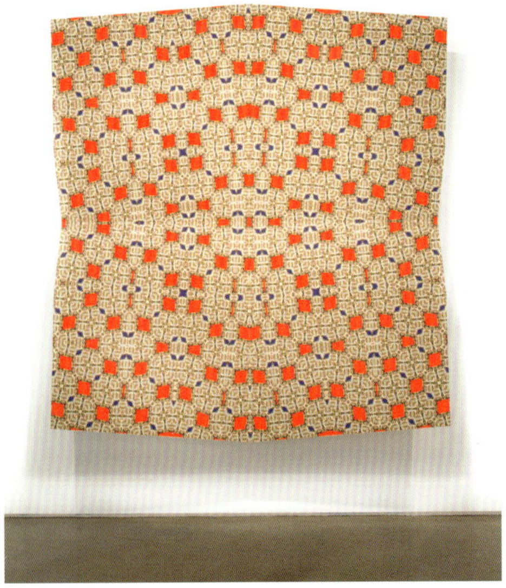

Sanaz Mazinani, *State Prism*, 2011
44 x 42 x 7 inch set of four photographs mounted
on dibond with custom wooden structure
Photograph by Adam Reich
Courtesy of the artist and Stephen Bulger Gallery

State Prism, 2011, is not an easy image to read, a faceted, multiplied, jumble of signifiers. At first the large photograph seems a brightly coloured fabric: a near-square with regular vermillion near-rectangles and smaller blue-mauve diamond shapes on a busy beige ground. The red rectangle at the centre is doubled and redoubled into 55 units of changing sizes and shapes in folded and flipped mirror images. The blue diamonds are in turn doubled and further mirrored across the glossy field, and the overall surface is opened up in quarters to stand slightly away from the wall. Subtly, these bright red and blue geometries deflect attention away from the tiny but more significant 'background' elements, their tunnelled perspectives spread out over the surface.

Looking more closely, one deciphers new details. A soldier stands stiffly on guard but 'at ease' in his sand-coloured fatigues, hands clasped behind his back, his face obscured by heavy black marker. A series of coffins is arranged behind him, each encased neatly in the red and white stripes of the American flag with tucked-away starred corners. All around are the curved struts and metal floor of an aircraft cargo carrier, a cave-like interior enclosing soldier and coffins in stilled, airless precision.

This prism or kaleidoscope is also a prison. To obscure his identity the soldier's face has been "redacted"—a literary term that once meant simply to edit, but now signals censoring for legal or security purposes. The soldier here is imprisoned in his sealed environment, accompanying casualties of war on their return home for burial. Other black markers fan out along edges—seating, perhaps—and additional soldiers are lined up in the rear, their blacked-out faces anonymous.

Under American President George Bush during the first Gulf war of 1990–91, it was made illegal to show images of wounded or dead American soldiers; the pictures here with their cancelled identities were released only after 2004 in response to demands made under the Freedom of Information Act. Danger and death were hidden away, smothered by dark marks in the interests of 'security' or simply to mask the numbers of war dead. Inner thoughts are equally muted in the suppression of public knowledge and smothering of individual response. War has been made 'safe'—always elsewhere and without casualties.

Any photograph requires selection, an image framed to focus on what is *inside* its borders, leaving everything else outside to be implied, imagined or ignored. Mazinani's prism-like refractions and splintered photomontages are painstaking digital collages, cut and pasted via Photoshop. Seams and edges are smoothed until invisible, the multiplied shapes becoming fabric-like, woven and printed. Like a Persian miniature or carpet, the time invested in *making* is matched by the care needed to *see*: to decode and evaluate. The ordered vortex of shapes leads to disequilibrium, disorientation, a pattern of captured light and colour braced by an almost floral geometry: multiple viewpoints for new voices.

Peggy Gale

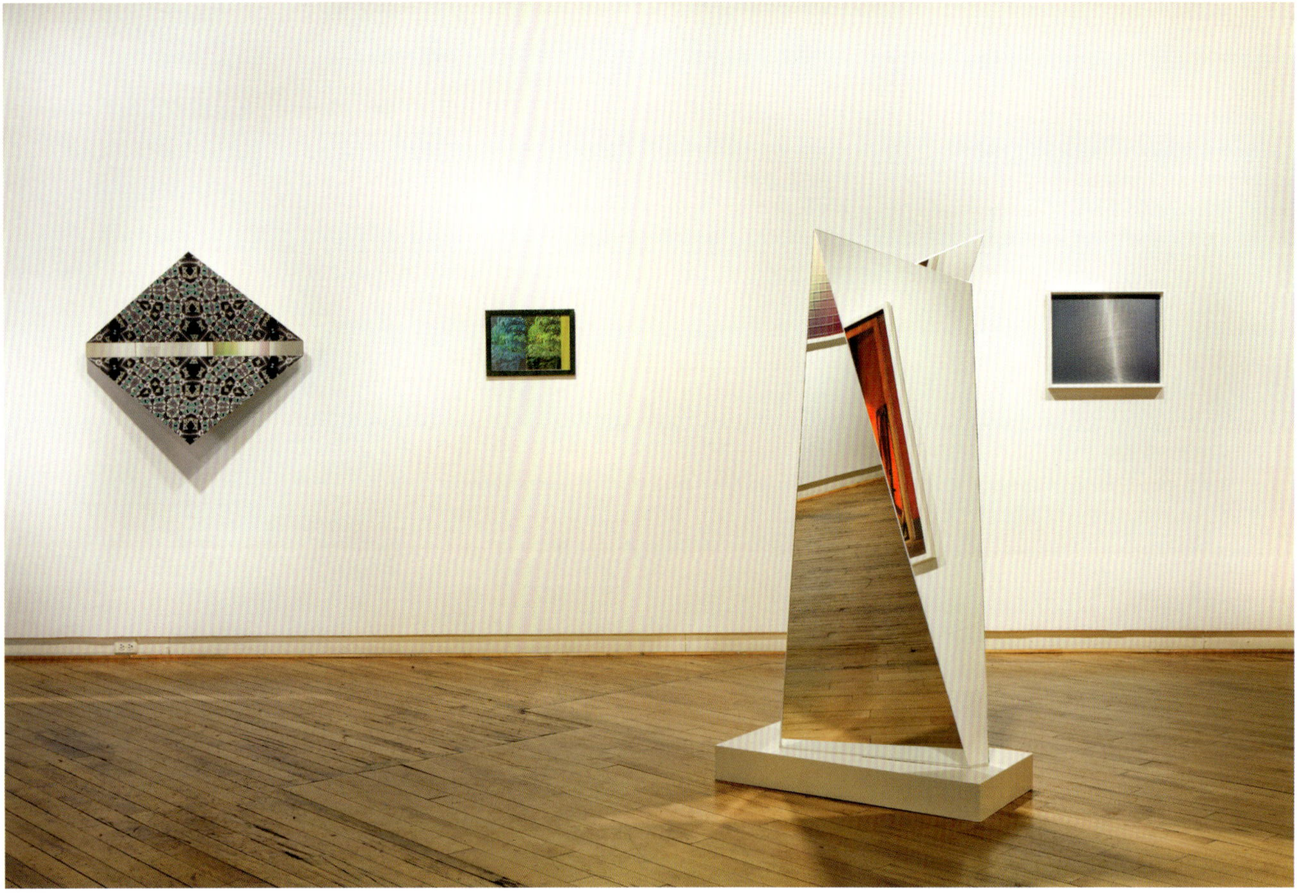

Sanaz Mazinani, installation view of the exhibition
"Site, Sight and Insight", Gallery 44 Centre for
Contemporary Photography, Toronto, 2014
Photograph by Morris Lum

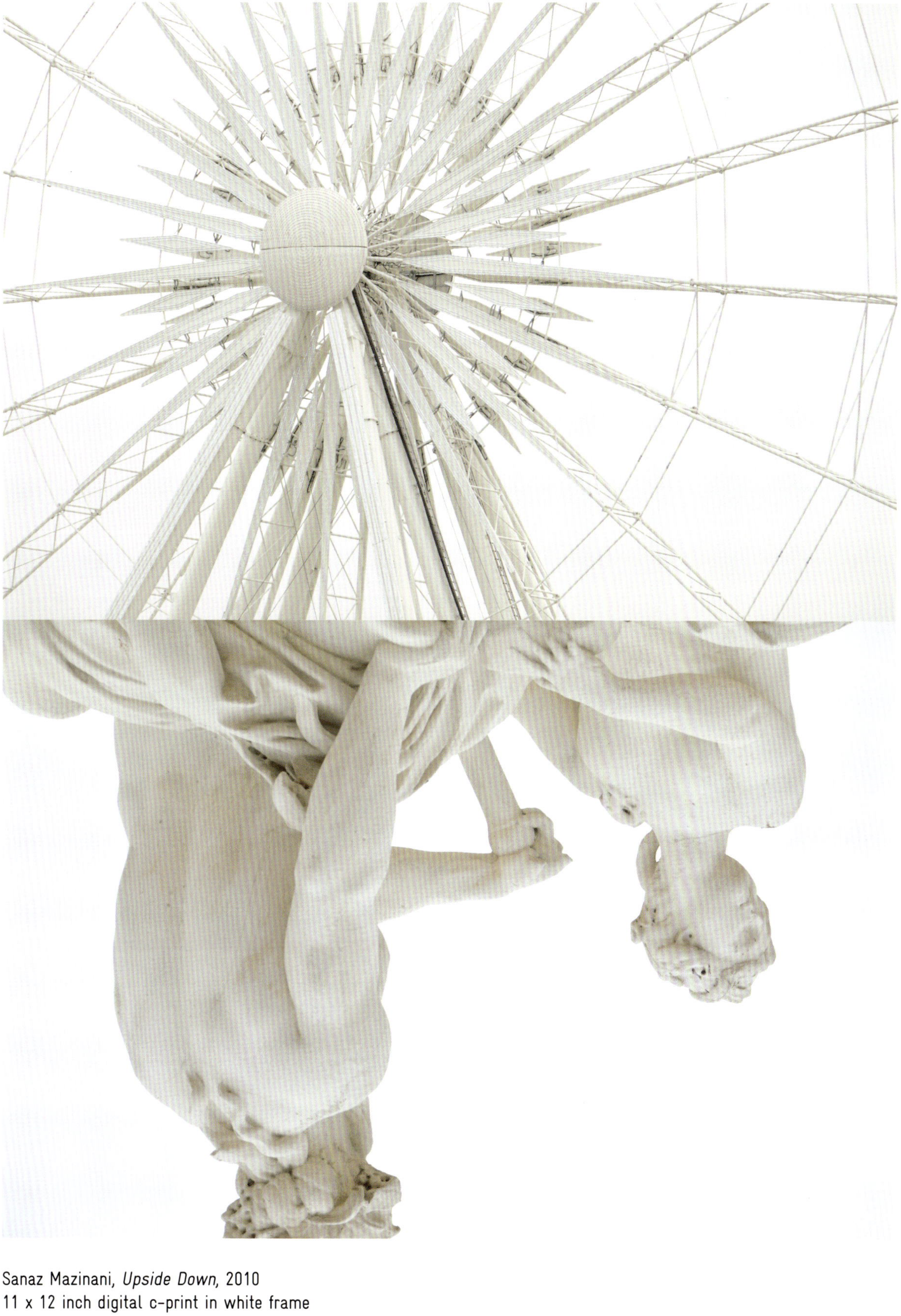

Sanaz Mazinani, *Upside Down*, 2010
11 x 12 inch digital c-print in white frame
Courtesy of the artist and Stephen Bulger Gallery

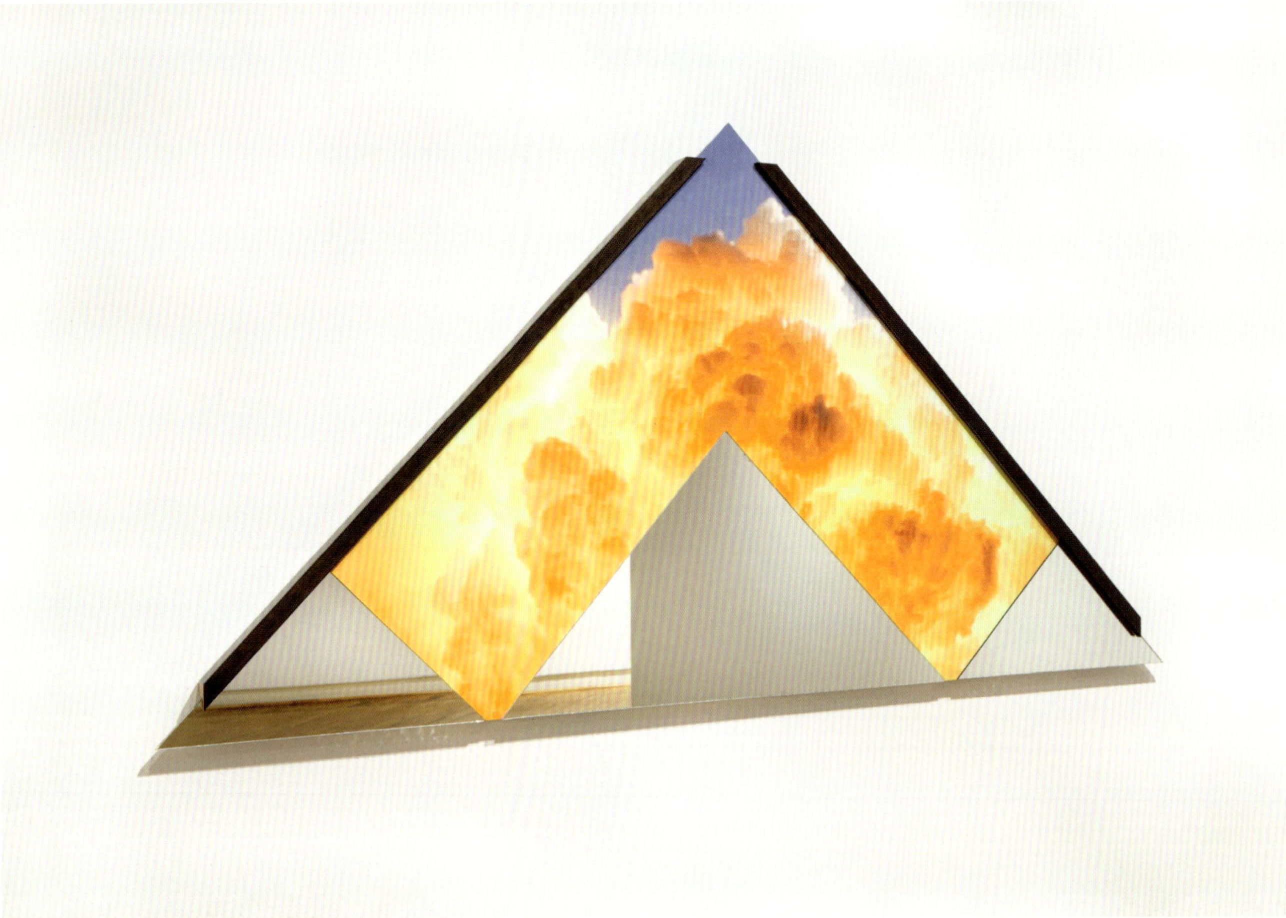

Sanaz Mazinani, installation documentation
Untitled #3, 26 x 52 inch pigment print with
mirror and wood, 2012–13
Photograph by Adam Reich
Courtesy of the artist and Stephen Bulger Gallery

When you look in the mirror, do you see yourself? Do you get caught up in your reflection, and all the lineages and histories buried in your features? Or does the mirror turn you outwards, to think of those whose faces are not your own? What does a reflection do?

Mirrors are generally figured as objects of isolation, the natural outcome of sinful vanity. (Narcissus didn't die at the hands of another, after all.) Writing about photography relies on this distinction: in 1978, John Szarkowski, then the Director of Photography at the Museum of Modern Art, argued that, "The photograph is seen either as a *mirror*—a romantic expression of the photographer's sensibility as it projects itself on the things and sights of this world; or as a *window*—through which the exterior world is explored in all its presence and reality."[1] But what if the mirror, with its admissions of subjectivity and partiality, actually presents a more accurate world than the window?

It isn't necessary to reach very far back in history to see the mirror, quite literally, turned as a frame onto the outside world. In the eighteenth century, artists who wanted to be a little more like Claude Lorrain carried around small, darkened convex mirrors. They could hold these so-called Claude glasses up to capture a landscape and find it readily framed in picturesque style.

Artists have always looked through glasses, darkly, but Sanaz Mazinani's approach strikes deeper.

Not content to simply flash mirrors on the external world, Mazinani turns her viewers outwards. In *Untitled #3*, 2012—13, she merges image, a mushrooming explosion of orange and yellow flames, and reflection. Approaching the work, viewers are plunged into the catastrophe's midst, with their very act of looking reflected back in sharp relief. In blending the documentary image and the reflection, Mazinani forces her viewers to recognize their own act of looking. There are echoes of Michael Snow here; Mazinani works "to make seeing palpable".[2]

While the Claude glasses offered a world made tame, Mazinani deploys her content to haunt. Taking a found image, she recasts the original framing of a well-worn category: engulfing flames that offer a metonymic gesture to disaster and warfare. This explosion is the stuff of photojournalistic reportage and AP Images, but Mazinani severs it from its source. Untethered from context, these flames exist only in relation to the viewers, who find themselves engulfed.

Mazinani manages to make the disaster image, so emptied out by its sheer ubiquity, new again. Or at least more relevant again to the viewer who finds themselves simultaneously in its midst and aware of its construction and mediation. She immolates her audience to force them outside of themselves.

Caoimhe Morgan-Feir

1. The Museum of Modern Art, *Mirrors + Windows: American Photography since 1960,* Press Release, 1978.
2. Snow, Michael, *Collected Writings of Michael Snow,* Waterloo, ON: Wilfrid Laurier University Press, 1994, pp 26–27.

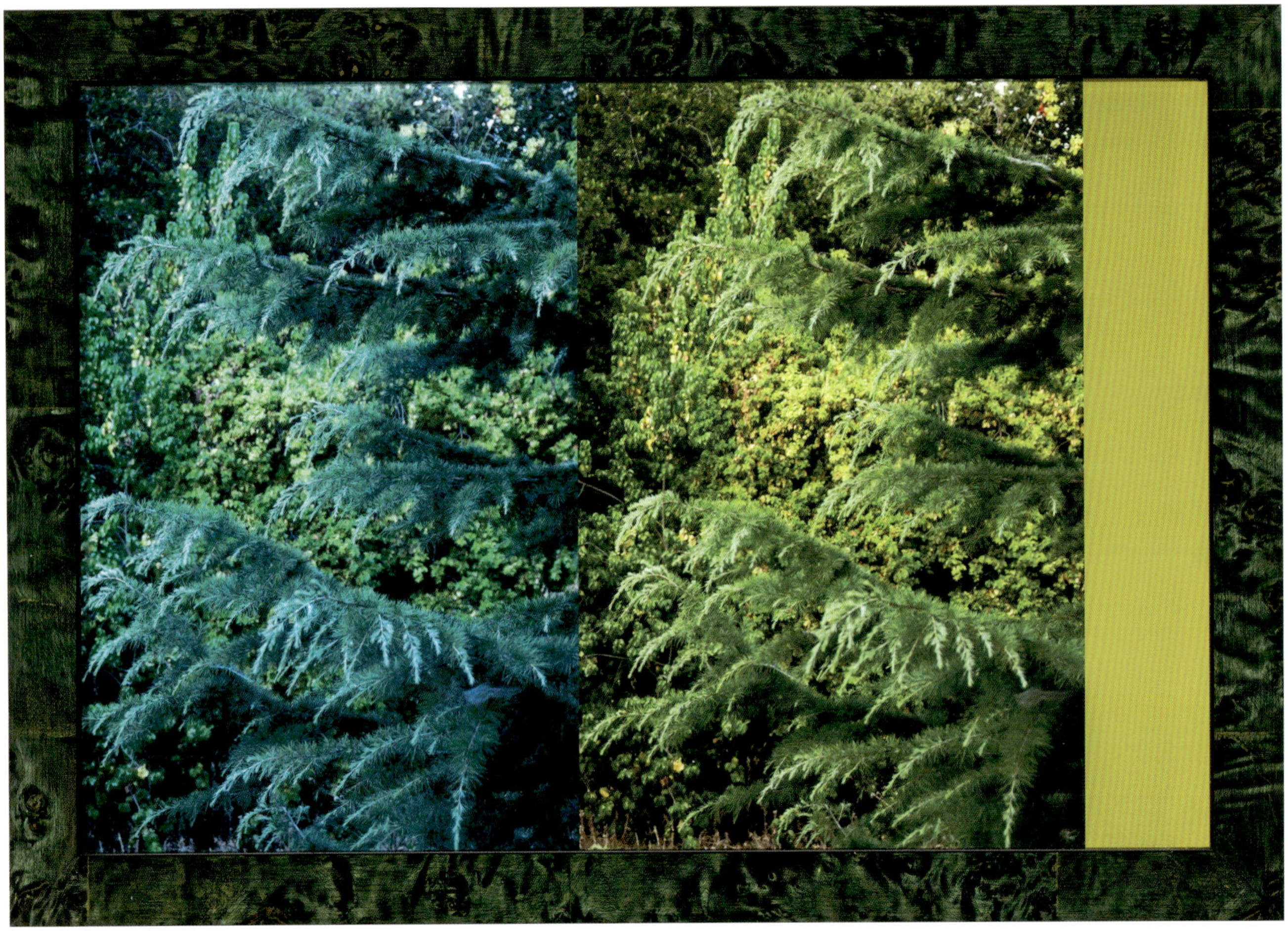

Sanaz Mazinani, *Landscape #27*, 2011
14 x 9 inch photographic collage
in custom hunter green frame
Courtesy of the artist and Stephen Bulger Gallery

Two trees, nearly identical, appear side by side in a hunter green wooden frame. Their elongated branches extend from beyond the frame, draped elegantly like the arms of a dancer reaching out towards the barre. My eyes dart back and forth between the two photographs, trying to puzzle out why—despite being the same image—they appear to be so different. The cool blue tones of the one on the left recall a film still from a moody psychological thriller. On the right, I see the warm, bright hues of a summer vacation snapshot. Both are there. Neither is right.

Sanaz Mazinani explores what it means to 'see' photographically: how changes in the effects of light, and in the camera's ability to register colour, alter our perception of the world and, in turn, our sense of place in it. The lone tree is, of course, a (clichéd) symbol of Canadian identity, and it is difficult at first not to read this image as a continuation of Mazinani's interest in the ways that national identities are represented through colour schemes, distorted, pixilated and delivered at crude low-resolution in Google image search results.[1] But when I look again, I begin to doubt that I know where this photograph is. There is something different about the light, and about the trees, than what I expect to see. They are lusher, richer, nearly Technicolor in their saturation. It is, instead, a photograph taken in California, shortly after Mazinani moved there: a study of the difference of light on the west coast compared to that in Toronto. The variations between the images are created by adjustments to the white balance in the camera: two ways the camera saw the same scene.

Our perceptual apparatus tends to correct for colour and light variations like these, but Mazinani's photographs delay and obstruct this process, asking which is the truthful representation of the tree, and raising the question of whether there is such a thing. The images's presentation, pasted next to one another, butted up against an abstract patch of olive green, and encased in a lush pattern that replicates the textures of the tree's needles and branches, further complicates the promise of photographic accuracy and the duplicity of photographic mimesis. To see Mazinani's twin trees is to see photography's unique capacities, and limitations, for registering the world and to wonder at what we cannot see when we look at photographs.

Gabrielle Moser

1. For *Digital Screens*, 2012, Mazinani experimented with the hues that were delivered by searching the word "Iraq" (warm earth tones of brown, green and red) and "USA". Heather, Rosemary, "Articulated Looking", *Sanaz Mazinani: Site, Sight, and Insight*, Toronto: Gallery 44, 2013.

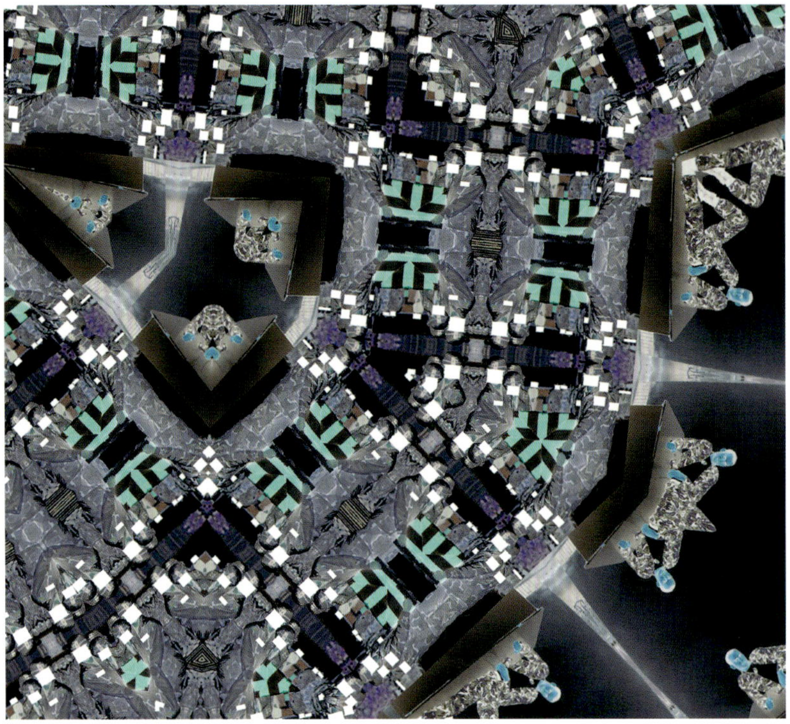

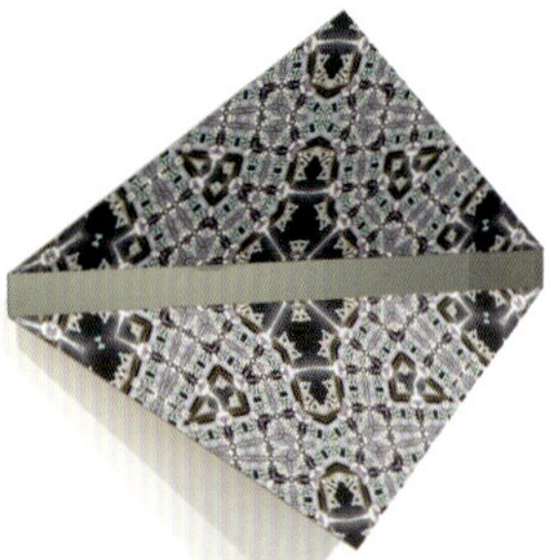

Sanaz Mazinani, *Redacted March #3*, 2013
set of two 17 x 42 inch pigment print with mirror
mounted on wooden subframe
Photograph by Adam Reich
Courtesy of the artist and Stephen Bulger Gallery

Sanaz Mazinani works covertly. Her photomosaics are dazzling and sleek; they marry the hard edges of military hardware and the geometric outlines of corporate logos with the elaborate patterns and brilliant colours of traditional Islamic ornaments. Her works are also overtly political, with images of warfare, rebellion, protest, and crass commercialism spliced together in unsettling pairings. Globalization, war, terrorism, multiculturalism, and sexism are always at play in Mazinani's work, but her true subjects are photography and the act of seeing.

Employing techniques such as collage, mirroring, inversion, decontextualization, and juxtaposition, she transforms photographs drawn from myriad sources until they are unrecognizable. This process of intense manipulation prods viewers to interrogate the nature of the images they are looking at—as well as their sources and the ideologies they are articulating—with varying degrees of subtlety.

Redacted March #3 may be one of the most intricate and bold pieces in Mazinani's series of patterned and kaleidoscopic works. It pairs an image, taken from the Department of Defense's website, of US soldiers carrying the coffin of a colleague killed in combat, with a photo that a young man took of himself posing in camouflage military fatigues and posted on Facebook. One image shows the solemn theatrics and fatal risks of war, while the other portrays military service as something far more casual, practically domestic, and potentially empowering. Mazinani has used negative images of both photos, further confounding viewers with a palette of turquoise, blue, grey, and silver that seems better suited to a science-fiction film. The result is an arresting and strange image that appears futuristic in its stretched, diamond-like shape—even more so with its central strip of mirror—yet labyrinthine and mysterious in its details. It has incredible visual power, but also demands close observation and diligent deciphering.

Mazinani's work aims to provoke greater visual literacy and a more sophisticated understanding of the increasingly image-based world through which we move. "Photographs provide evidence, but are not reality", she has said. Understanding that distinction has become an essential skill for successful navigation in the twenty-first century. This more complex and fluid way of interpreting photographic images was taken up very successfully in the International Center of Photography's 2013 Triennial, an exhibition that did not include Mazinani's work but very well could have. "[W]e initially thought of calling the exhibition 'Chaos'", the Triennial's curators wrote in their catalogue introduction. "However, we became increasingly convinced that the present moment is not one of incomprehensible disorder, but is instead witnessing the emergence of a new kind of order, one shaped by identifiable social, political, and technological changes."[1] By imposing complex, sometimes counterintuitive systems and patterns onto the chaotic visual culture of our time, Mazinani's photomosaics show how malleable and empowering this new order can be.

Benjamin Sutton

1. Lehan, Joanna, Kristen Lubben, Christopher Phillips, et al, *A Different Kind Of Order: The ICP Triennial*, New York/London: Prestel, 2013.

STUDIO

Sheree Hovsepian and Brea Souders

Karsten Lund

Aura Seikkula

Kate Steciw

Darren Campion

Mark Durant

Arianne Di Nardo

Ray Gilliar

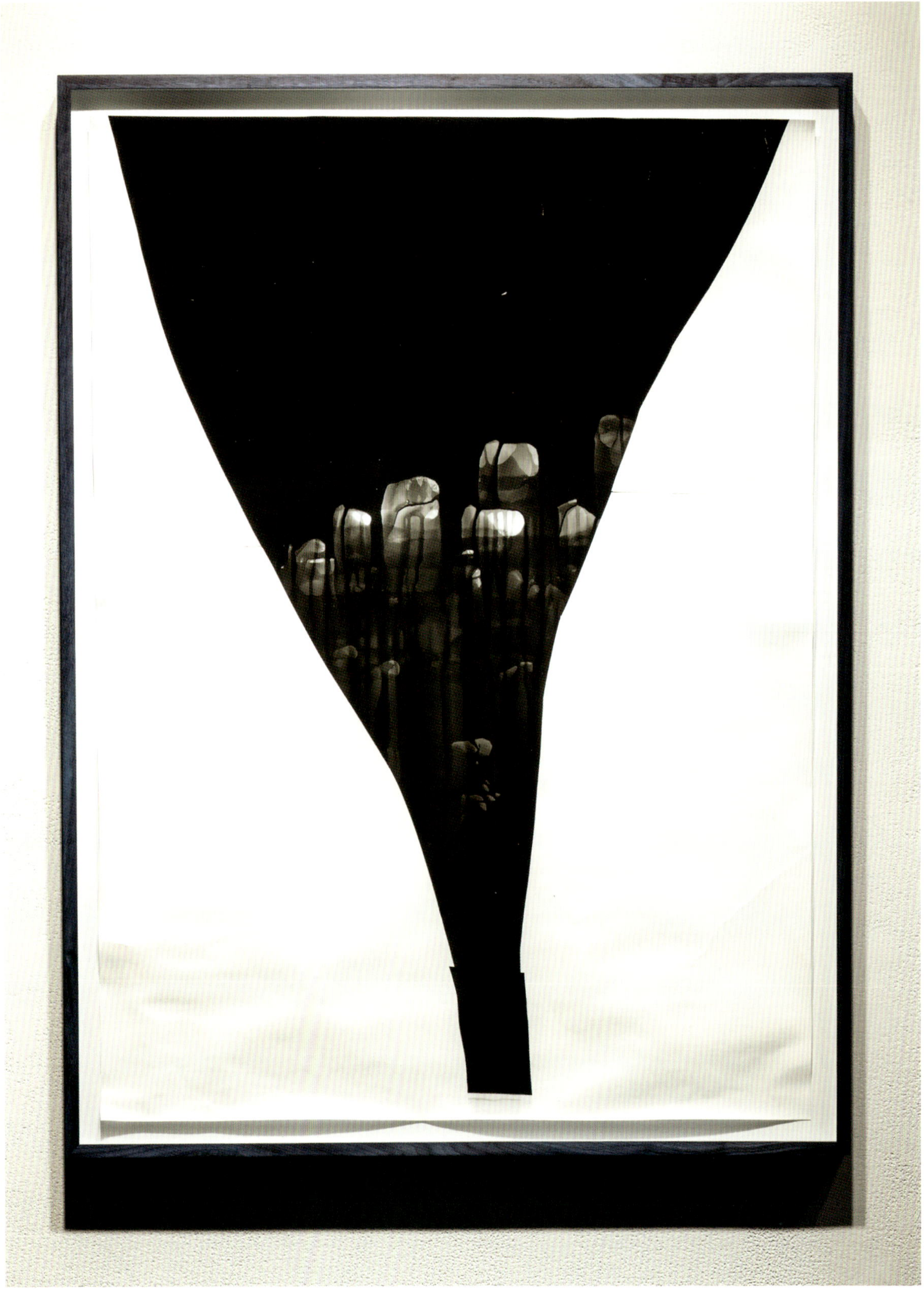

Sheree Hovsepian, *Deluge*, 2014
43 x 32 inch unique silver gelatin photogram
Photograph by Toni Hafkenscheid
Courtesy of the artist and Monique Meloche Gallery

In a town or city somewhere a dark room is soaked in a muted red dusk; the sound of running water and a vague aroma, acrid and pungent in places, gathers in its corners like signs of another dark world drifting up from subterranean depths. If you close your eyes and embrace a misperception, this room could be a cave far below the surface of the earth, accessible only by time-carved passageways and an hour's stony crawl into the ground. (How many rooms like this still exist—not the cave, but this room of tables and devices, a remainder of another era that hasn't entirely disappeared?)

In this peculiar tinted darkness, an artist spends hours pouring and re-pouring chemicals, letting her eyes adjust, coaxing sheets of paper with subtle shifts of her hands, mulling over the properties of liquids, the latency of silver salts, invisible until certain procedures take place, and gradually growing attuned to the residual weight of vanished light and its transfigured reappearance in the dark.

If all goes well, she can count on the slight shivering power of an accident—the not-quite expected outcome. A fissure splits open. The shadows part and gather again. Water falls and stalagmites rise—or so it appears—coming from nowhere.

Peel back the white surface. Draw back the curtain. Beneath the paper is a mantle made of something denser yet immaterial, fired into being by photons, minerals and chance. Beneath the paper is an endless crevice, inviting us into the numinous heart of the earth. And somewhere in there is another darkness, too, a humid echo of all the dark rooms you've ever known and all those yet to come.

"In the dark", Don DeLillo writes, "the mind runs on like a devouring machine, the only thing awake in the universe".

Recount for us then all the dark rooms you've known. Start with the one where you fall asleep every night (or the one you flee for other bedrooms). The one that floats in the air before a movie begins—which is different from the one after it ends. Maybe the room that went abruptly black when the power grid died that humid summer. If you've been inside a cave, add that one, too, and leave ample space for all those you've forgotten or conflated over time.

Today every digital screen, like the one on which I write, is a mineshaft with an alien glow within its walls, a perpetual light at the end of its endless tunnel. The dwindling world of analogue photography, however, while ruled by the laws of light, carries within itself its opposite, a lightless-ness foreshadowed in the dark rooms where photos are made (or used to be), in the black cloths draped over old cameras. The fact remains that in this world the brightest light, unobstructed, yields the deepest blacks.

In a dark room, in that universe, an artist finds new fractures and fault lines in a photograph's pale silver-ridden body. An entrance to the earth. A gray luminescence waiting in the paper. Underneath its skin is a cavernous diamond, whose depths we cannot reach, a fissure for the eye and for the mind, that great devouring machine.

Karsten Lund

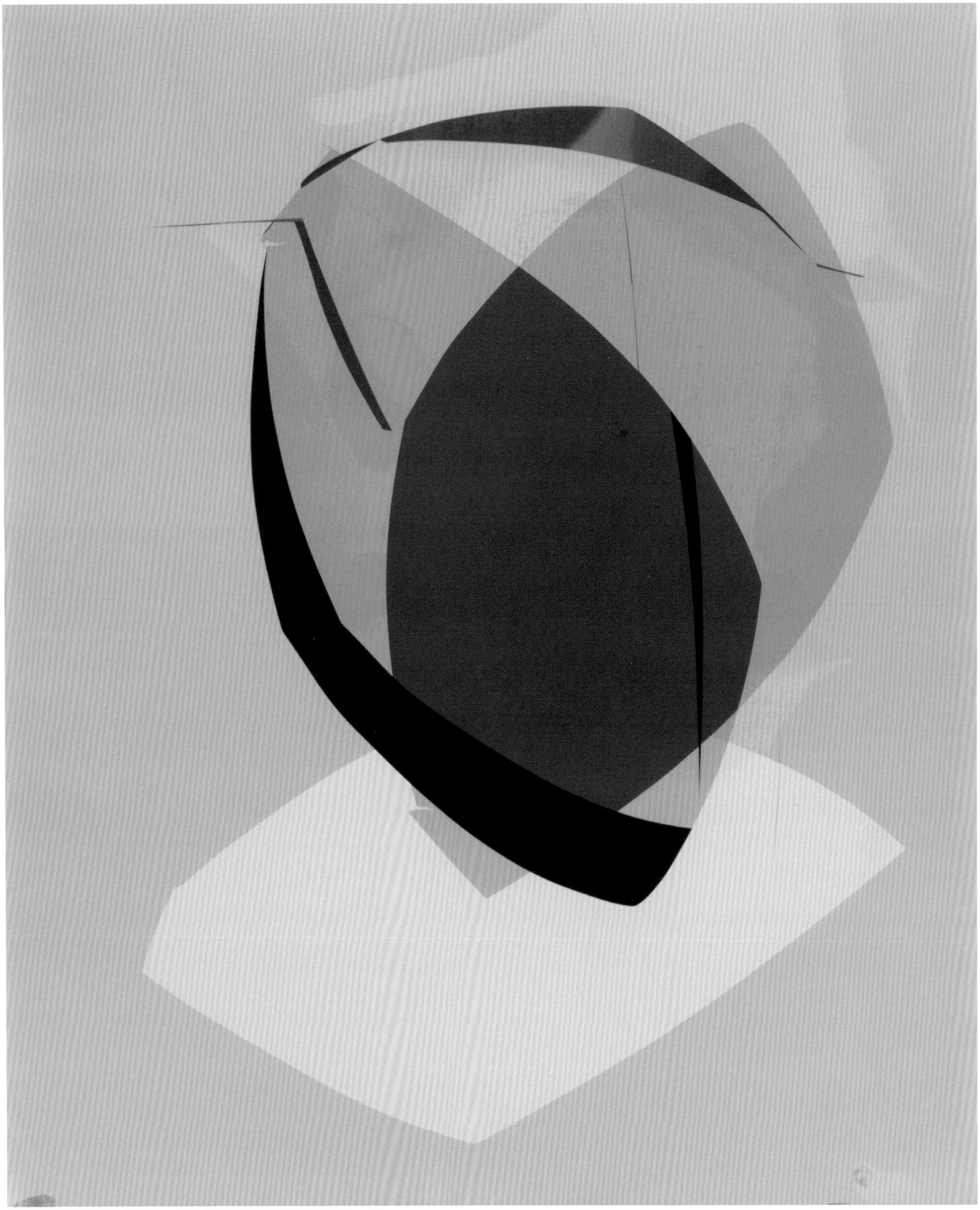

Sheree Hovsepian, *Untitled #20*, 2012
from the series *Haptic Wonders*, 20 x 24 inch
unique silver gelatin photogram
Courtesy of the artist and Monique Meloche Gallery

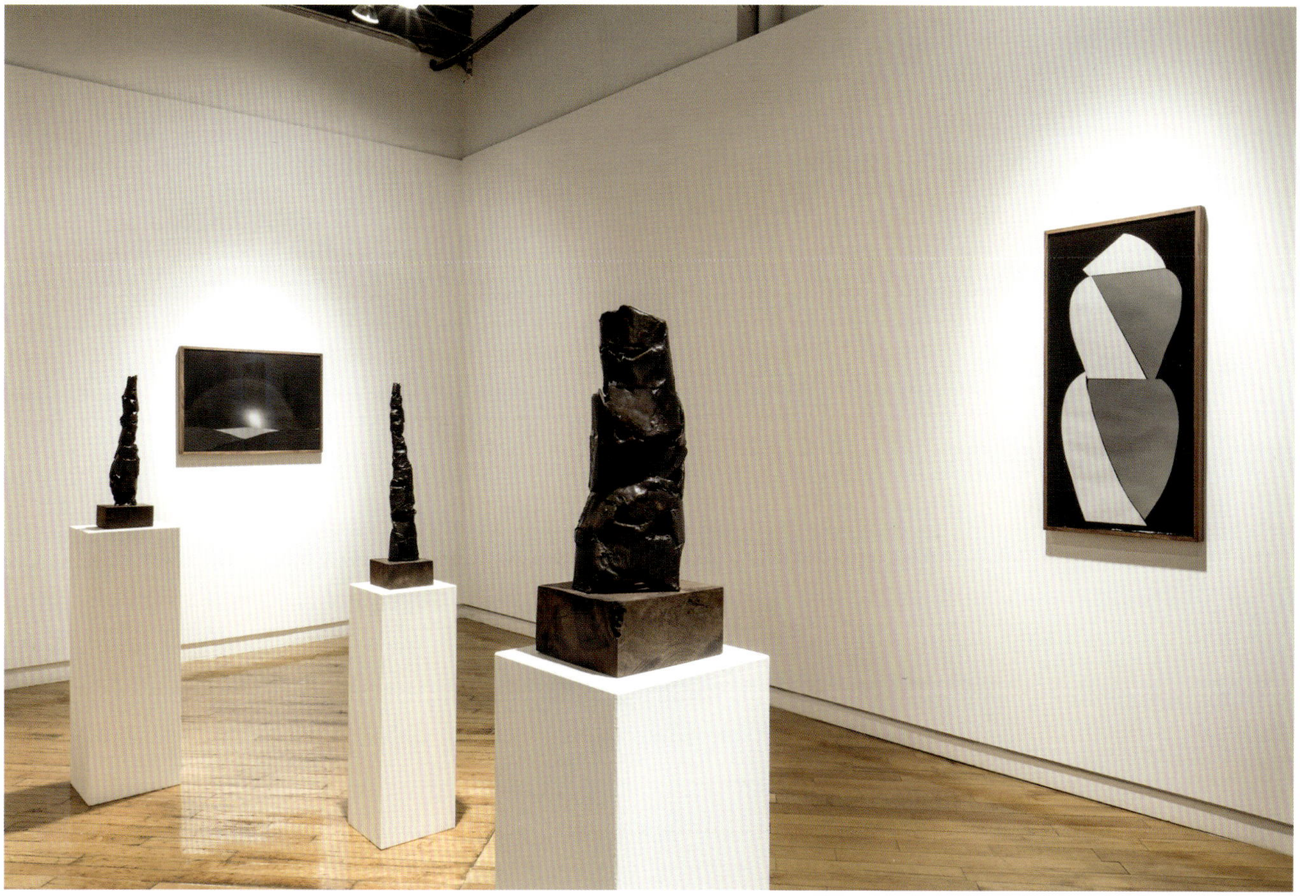

Sheree Hovsepian, installation view of the exhibition "Soft Landing", Gallery 44 Centre for Contemporary Photography, Toronto, 2014
Photograph by Toni Hafkenscheid
Courtesy of the artist and Monique Meloche Gallery

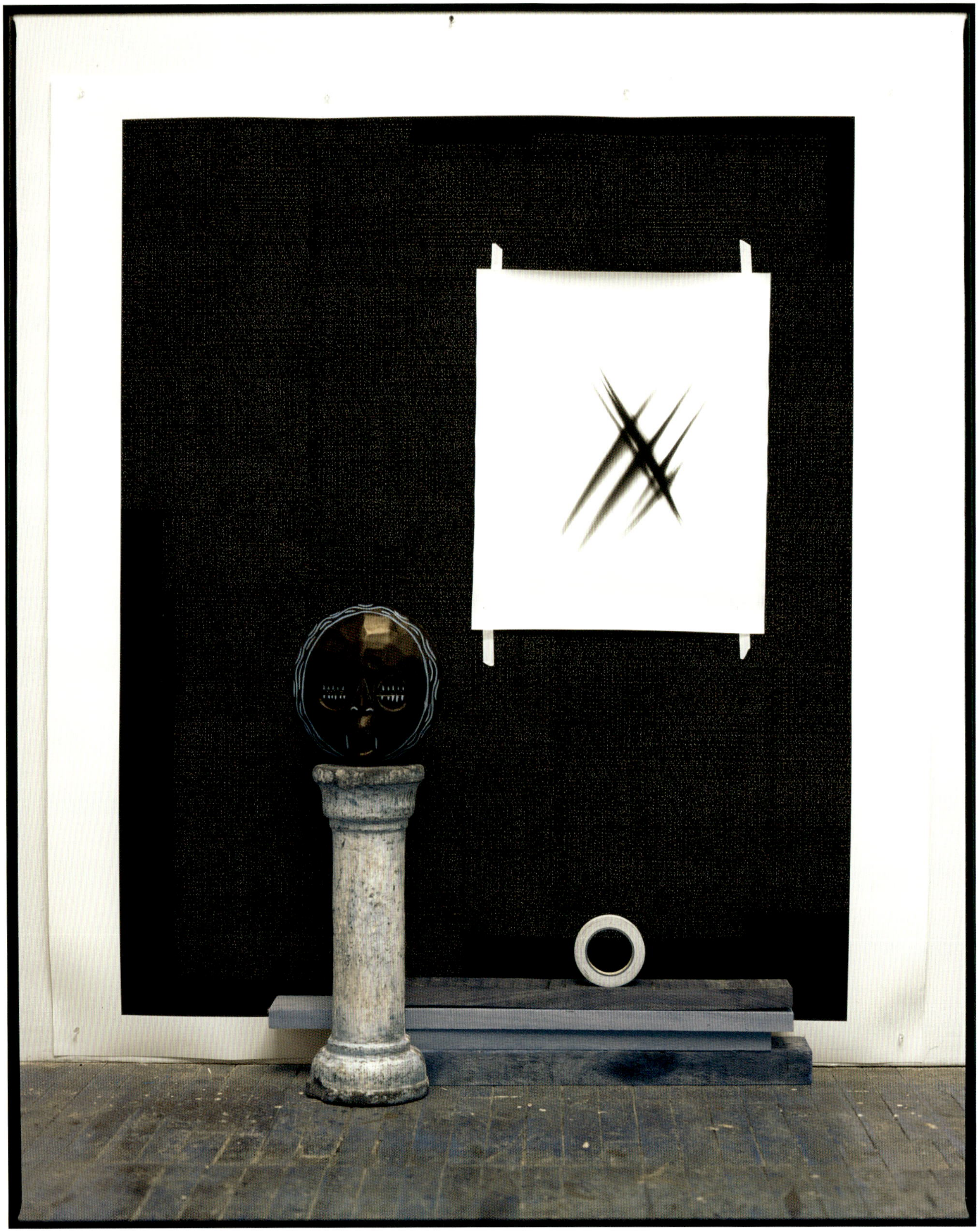

Sheree Hovsepian, *Studio Assemblage 1,* 2014
30 x 40 inch custom archival pigment print
Courtesy of the artist and Monique Meloche Gallery

REPEAT REPEATED

In our immediate surroundings, repetition can be seen as a construct that maintains order and creates structured systems that inform everyday patterns. Whether ritualized products of a behaviour or arrangements of structural bureaucracy, repetition is a kind of ebb and flow that maintains social equilibrium. We compose our days through repetitious acts. The resulting metanarratives that arise through these mundane cycles—and our understanding of these narratives—are defined through each individual repetition.

Sheree Hovsepian troubles this rhythm by focusing in on objects and images, by enabling a process focused on variation.

Hovsepian pays close attention to the particulars of production and expresses a commitment to the power of a single object or image. While her assemblages are constructed within her studio, she is not aiming for site-specificity. Instead, her assemblages convey the possibility of their medium. Rather than underlining or reciting one possible narrative strategy, Hovsepian employs various visual stagings in order to trace the context of an image, the medium of an image and the display of an image. Enabled by her studio practice, the meaning of an image varies from cultural artefact to analogies for the politics of display and exhibition.

Interestingly, Hovsepian attempts to make visual a kind of system of reciprocity, where contribution to the process is an invitation to renew and review features and attributes within and beyond that practice. With this endeavour she depicts various symbolic and cultural signifiers, which are collected, decontextualized and relocated in, and alongside, experimental presentation methodologies.

Prolonging the results of her process, Hovsepian contradicts generic attitudes towards production, ones focused on final outcomes. She employs a temporary, almost disposable approach, where variables are inevitably replaced; with a dedicated attempt to continually revise and rethink. By exploring the strategies of presentation, she demonstrates that the production of artworks is never truly finite.

Aura Seikkula

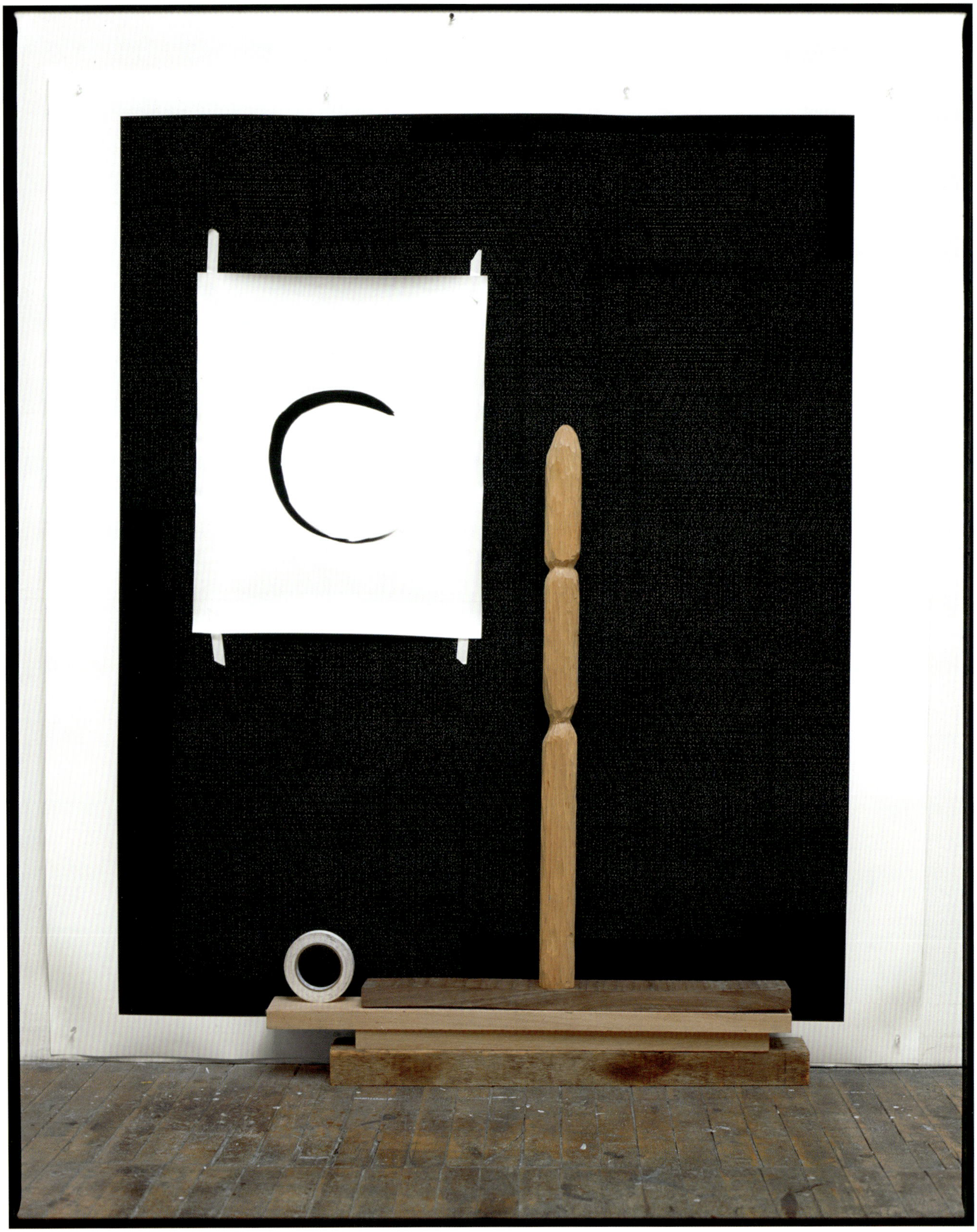

Sheree Hovsepian, *Studio Assemblage 2,* 2014
30 x 40 inch custom archival pigment print
Courtesy of the artist and Monique Meloche Gallery

That distant city is forming.
They returned there every day.
Unaware of its stability.

We have been up all night, my friends and I, beneath mosque lamps whose brass cupolas are as bright as our souls, because like them they were illuminated by the internal glow of electric hearts. And trampling underfoot our native sloth on opulent Persian carpets, we have been discussing right up to the limits of logic and scrawling the paper with demented writing.

Future as our witness.
Eminently bold.
An antagonistic libretto bellows.

Our hearts were filled with an immense pride at feeling ourselves standing quite alone, like lighthouses or like the sentinels in an outpost, facing the army of enemy stars encamped in their celestial bivouacs.

"Come, my friends!" I said. "Let us go! At last Mythology and the mystic cult of the ideal have been left behind. We are going to be present at the birth of the centaur and we shall soon see the first angels fly! We must break down the gates of life to test the bolts and the padlocks! Let us go! Here is the very first sunrise on earth! Nothing equals the splendour of its red sword which strikes for the first time in our millennial darkness."

Why would you desert the impossible race.
The command in their demand.
The world in our hands. The world where we land.

Let the good incendiaries with charred fingers come! Here they are! Heap up the fire to the shelves of the libraries! Divert the canals to flood the cellars of the museums! Let the glorious canvases swim ashore! Take the picks and hammers! Undermine the foundation of venerable towns!

Ignore the past.
There is no return.
But would you even remember.
When we ask.

But we shall not be there. They will find us at last one winter's night in the depths of the country in a sad hangar echoing with the notes of the monotonous rain, crouched near our trembling aeroplanes, warming our hands at the wretched fire which our books of today will make when they flame gaily beneath the glittering flight of their pictures.

And the images, the ones you agreed to draw
Are shattered, to be eaten and built no more.
Burn the words and there you will meet.

They will crowd around us, panting with anguish and disappointment, and exasperated by our proud indefatigable courage, will hurl themselves forward to kill us, with all the more hatred as their hearts will be drunk with love and admiration for us.

Look at us! We are not out of breath, our hearts are not in the least tired.

Aura Seikkula (in italics) in dialogue with excerpts from FT Marinetti, *Futurist Manifesto*, 1909. Translation from Joll, James, *Three Intellectuals in Politics*, New York, Pantheon, 1961, pp 179–184.

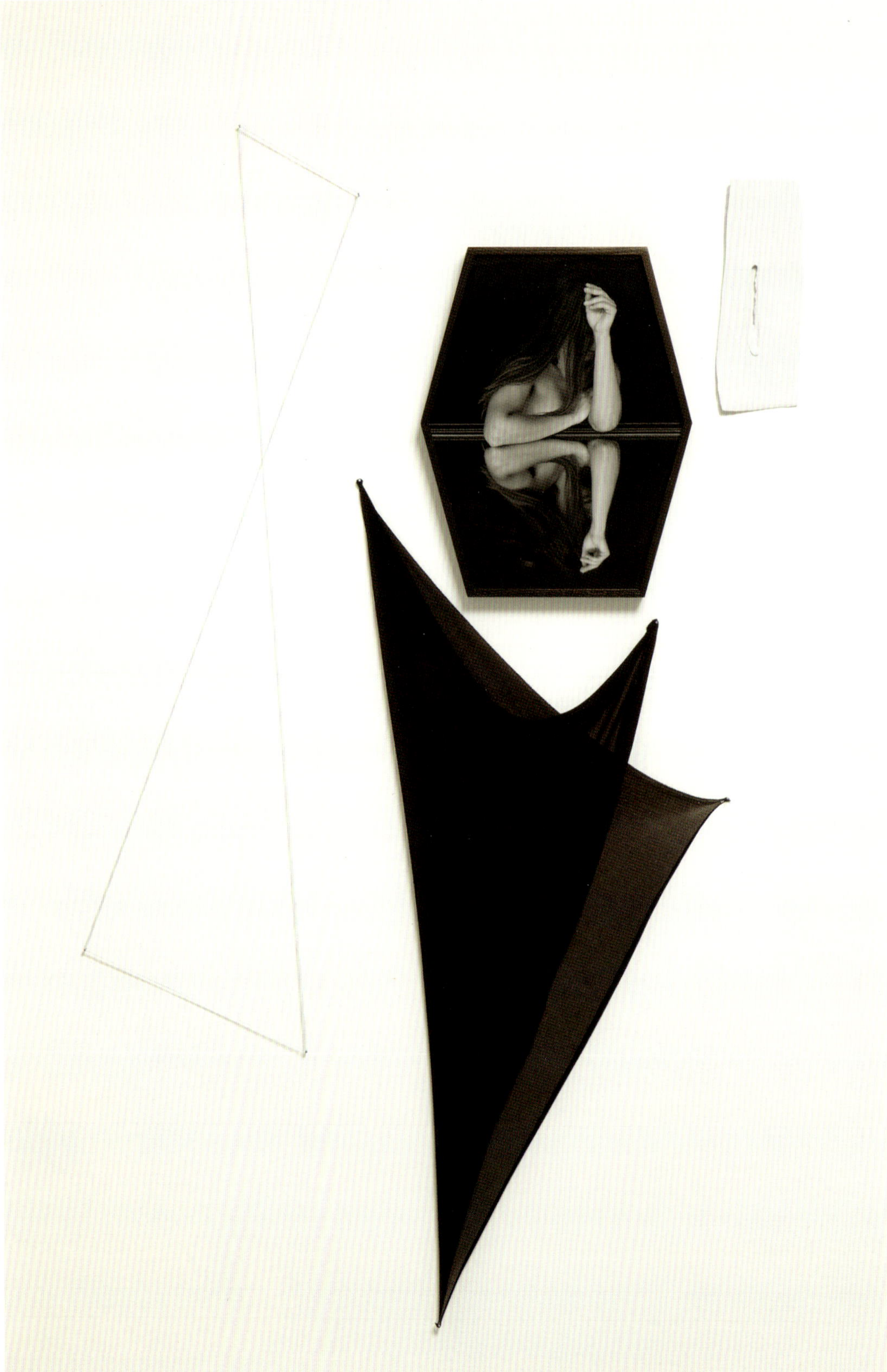

Sheree Hovsepian, *Material Gesture #1 (Sister)*, 2012
framed silver gelatin photograph, porcelain, fabric,
string, nails (dimensions variable)
Courtesy of the artist and Monique Meloche Gallery

Sister. She is like one to me in many ways. Over ten years gone since we shared two icy and tumultuous years in Chicago, our friendship forged in the crucible of lousy art, deep dish pizza, late nights in drafty apartments and later nights in cramped and cluttered studios. There were eight of us, five of us inseparable. We five were bound by a distinct but undefinable unease about the medium we'd chosen to study: photography. We writhed under the yoke of a system quickly outrunning itself. We witnessed the twin towers crumble on a computer screen yet a slide library and a colour processor less than a block away bore testament to an era quickly slipping from relevance or recognition.

It's nearly 12 years on now. Marriages have come and some have gone, children have been born, learned to walk and speak, we've lost parents and friends, made homes and through it all, made work.

It's a chilly afternoon and I'm having one of the best/worst years of my life. My face is swollen from crying when Sheree answers the door. She can tell. We quickly fall into conversation despite the fact we've not seen each other in months. That conversation on my end ebbs when I get my bearings and look around her space. It's a relief to be in her space, her real space and not some digital effigy. There are surfaces and surface tensions, interventions and interruptions and all seems in a state of interminable flux, which is invigorating to be around.

I'm handling a semi-hewn piece of wood, "Are you whittling?" I like to think of her whittling. "Yeah, I find this wood around the neighbourhood and I work on it, it's relaxing, nothing in mind, just mark-making". Perfect. That's all we, any of us, are trying to do anyway, right?

Around the studio there are other actions and objects acted on but they take different shapes, tending toward and away from varying states of entropy; a painted piece of felt, a photogram with pinholes interrupting its otherwise pristine surface, an African mask, photographs of these objects arranged and rearranged to be photographed again. Nothing is static. Forms echo other forms and fall back in on themselves to create new forms. The practice and the space are life affirming in this way.

Sheree has sisters by blood. Their bodies have entered her practice over the years as both subject and object, referential and referenced. It seems fitting in a practice so innately tuned to the strange alchemy of material transience to borrow from the bodies and bones of ones kin; as if by some transmutation, the force of their existence can be hewn or honed into an object that could potentially outlive us all. These are hopeful gestures, imbued with a kind of mystical reverence for both body and byproduct. One gets the sense that a mere representation will no longer do.

Kate Steciw

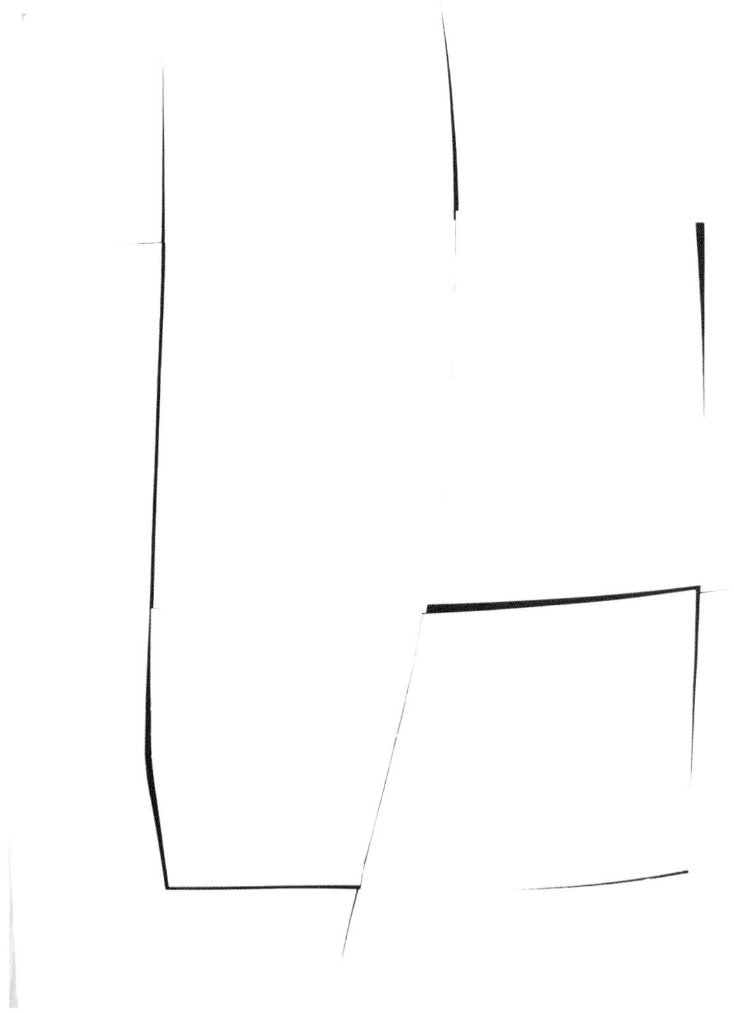

Sheree Hovsepian, *Untitled #88*, 2013
from the series *Haptic Wonders*, 20 x 24 inch
unique silver gelatin photogram
Courtesy of the artist and Monique Meloche Gallery

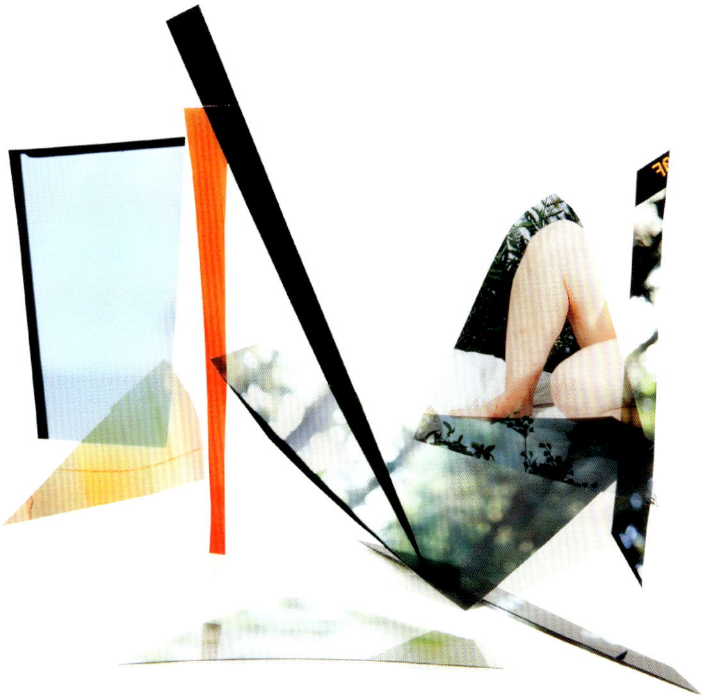

Brea Souders, *Film Electric #38*, 2013
archival inkjet print (dimensions variable)
Courtesy of the artist and Bruce Silverstein Gallery, NY

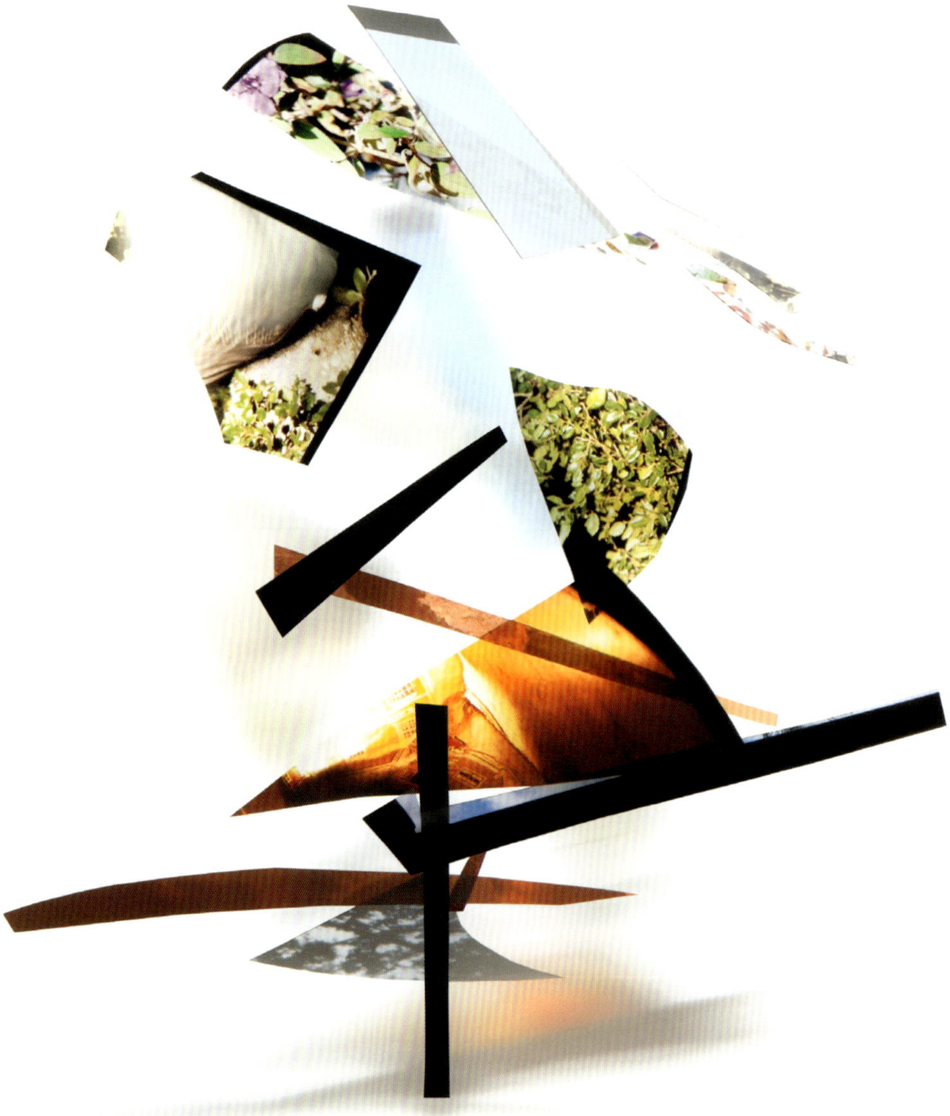

Brea Souders, *Film Electric #24*, 2013
archival inkjet print (dimensions variable)
Courtesy of the artist and Bruce Silverstein Gallery, NY

In looking at photographs we essentially look through or beyond them, neglecting the frame as a device that shapes our attention. This sense of ambiguity has been further widened by the prevalence of digital technologies, which make our encounter with images an ever more seamless and transparent experience. Rather than just being a discrete, tactile object, a photograph is now also a flow of information to be consumed, constantly in motion. The fragmentation of photographic media is at least one of the themes addressed by Brea Souders in this image and, indeed, the body of work from which it comes. Slicing into (what was once) the basic material of the medium to produce a literal description of photography as multiple atomized flows, she creates a sort of momentary collage in real space. But this fleeting arrangement has, in turn, been brought back to the photographic—it becomes in itself something that can only be seen photographically, describing the substance of time and light.

Just as the fractured space of Cubism, for example, was a way of visualizing the social and technological upheavals of the early twentieth century, so too do the shifting planes we see here seem like the embodiment of our own transformed encounter with photography, while still retaining the conventional frame as a sort of formal continuity within these exceptional changes. The 'content' of each fragment is less meaningful than the apparent disunity of their overall impression, a seemingly random distribution of partial impressions shorn of context. But the discontinuous space within the frame also brings our eye back to the surface of the image, activating our awareness of what is not usually—or easily—seen: the photograph itself. At the same time, the multiple and often clashing perspectives of the photographic fragments offer a sense of incompleteness that can never be shaped into a coherent view of the world; neither is it possible to trace the impression we have from each fragment back to whatever the 'whole' image might have been.

The point here is not a reductive concern with the material properties of photography as such. Souders's engagement with the medium is an inquiry into its uses, the burdens of seeing and remembering that no incarnation of the photograph can ever fully satisfy. Further to the implicit rejection of a singular view, the play of these suggestive fragments within the frame is a testament to the mobile dimensions of memory, where nothing is ever still. Seeing and knowing are fundamentally acts of synthesis; what they produce is not merely given, but is shaped according to specific conditions. The way in which we see the world, then, results from how our experience of it is organized. Souders is exposing the unstable landscape shared by our perceptions and the intangible means of digital technology.

This is not an elegiac work, motivated by a sentimental attachment to the supposed authenticity of analogue processes. Instead it considers the point of transition between very different realms, as a sort of compromise between where photography has been and where it is headed.

Darren Campion

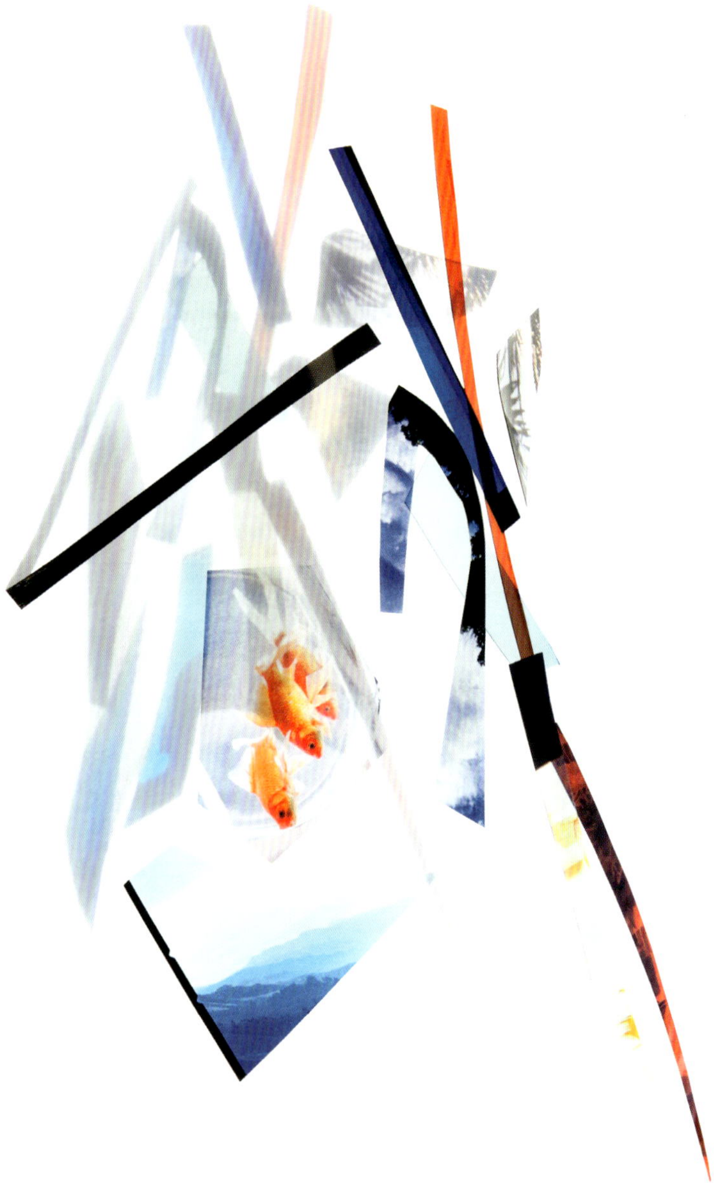

Brea Souders, *Film Electric #37*, 2013
archival inkjet print (dimensions variable)
Courtesy of the artist and Bruce Silverstein Gallery, NY

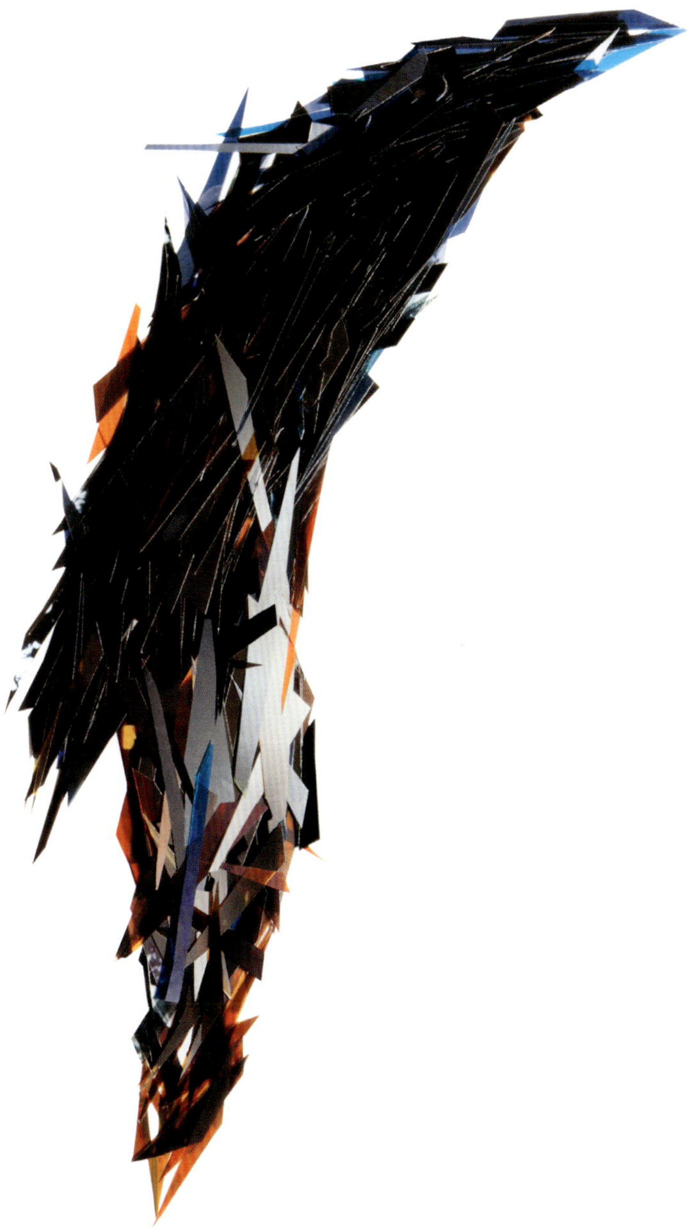

Brea Souders, *Mountains Without Faces #15*, 2013
archival inkjet print (dimensions variable)
Courtesy of the artist and Bruce Silverstein Gallery, NY

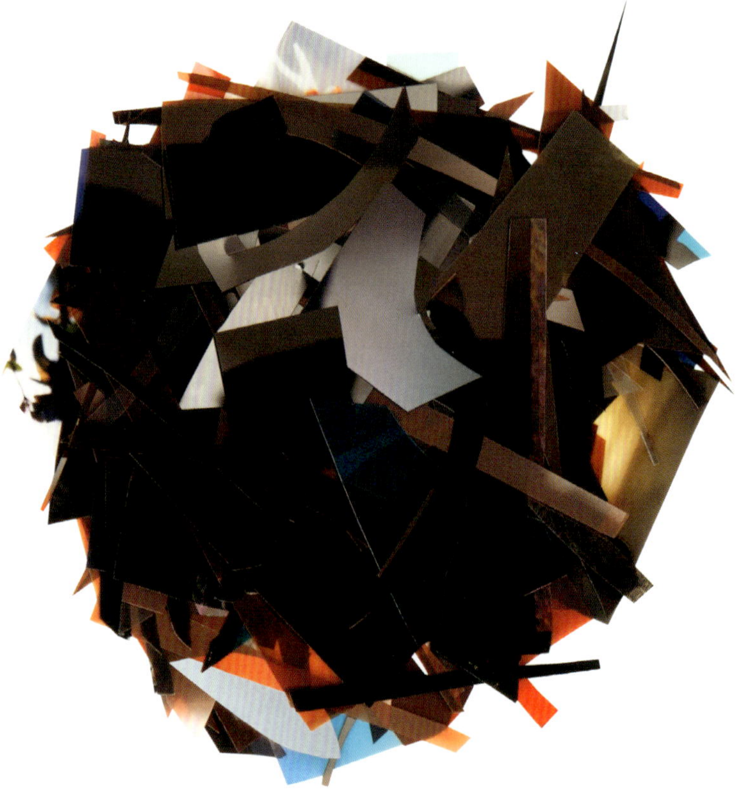

Brea Souders, *Mountains Without Faces #14*, 2013
archival inkjet print (dimensions variable)
Courtesy of the artist and Bruce Silverstein Gallery, NY

She walked down the sloping path toward her studio in the after-dinner dark, the taste of soupy flan still on her tongue. The waxing moon overhead was playing hide and seek with the tall pines and the loosely knotted blanket of clouds sliding in from the east. The old batteries in her flashlight could produce only a faint beam that nodded up and down in unison with her steps. She kicked stones as a warning to any nearby skunks, goblins or the rare black bear that sometimes passed through the woods in this part of New Hampshire. At a sudden rustle she directs the beam to the side of the path where she thinks she catches sight of a raccoon's tail scampering away through the underbrush. She isn't sure if she saw anything really, but was certain she would remember the image and in that case there was little difference between illusion and actuality.

Once inside the studio she switched on all the lights, bouncing floodlights off the cathedral ceiling, turning on desk lamps and even the nightlight in the bathroom. Like an emphatic response to nocturnal blindness, she created an internal sun; barely a shadow could escape the scattering illumination. Reflecting some of the wayward light about ten feet outside the north-facing windows, a stand of paper-white birch trees looked like pale and nervous tendrils reaching for the forest canopy. Photography is all about light of course, but in her images, light was not just a tool but a presence, a character, an obliterating force or benevolent companion, an energy that intersected with human affairs but took no fixed position in the ancient binary of good and bad.

She stood above her worktable and began to cut up old negatives and slide film, allowing the slivers of silver and dye to fall randomly. With occasional pangs of indecision, she remembers each image as the scissor blades sliced through the legs of a young woman, the ear of a bunny, or the sturdy stems of forsythia. Shards of underexposed frames, light-leaked edges, awkward compositions, and redundant poses, drop like petals into discarded bouquets. Sometimes the fragments spread across the paper in a manner that reminded her of photographic hieroglyphics communicating from a space in between image and mark. At other times the pieces clung together via static electricity, gathering in tight clusters to create dense and opaque geometries with bits of transparency jutting out around the edge. Her actions straddled photography's analogue past and its digital future, but she did not want to force a predetermined meaning and instead hoped to discover one. She wanted photography to be more than just a window pointing to something else; she hoped these chance arrangements might sing a new song.

Sensing the night had almost passed, and the glow of the outside would soon compete with that of the inside, she switched off all the lights and turned toward the wall of north-facing windows. Obscuring the view upon the lightening sky but still dark woods were hundreds of Luna Moths clinging to the surface of the glass. Filling the window frames to the edge, their furry white bodies sprouted enormous yet graceful pale green wings with eye-shaped markings that seemed to be staring at her expectantly, fluttering in a slow-motion plea for entry.

Mark Durant

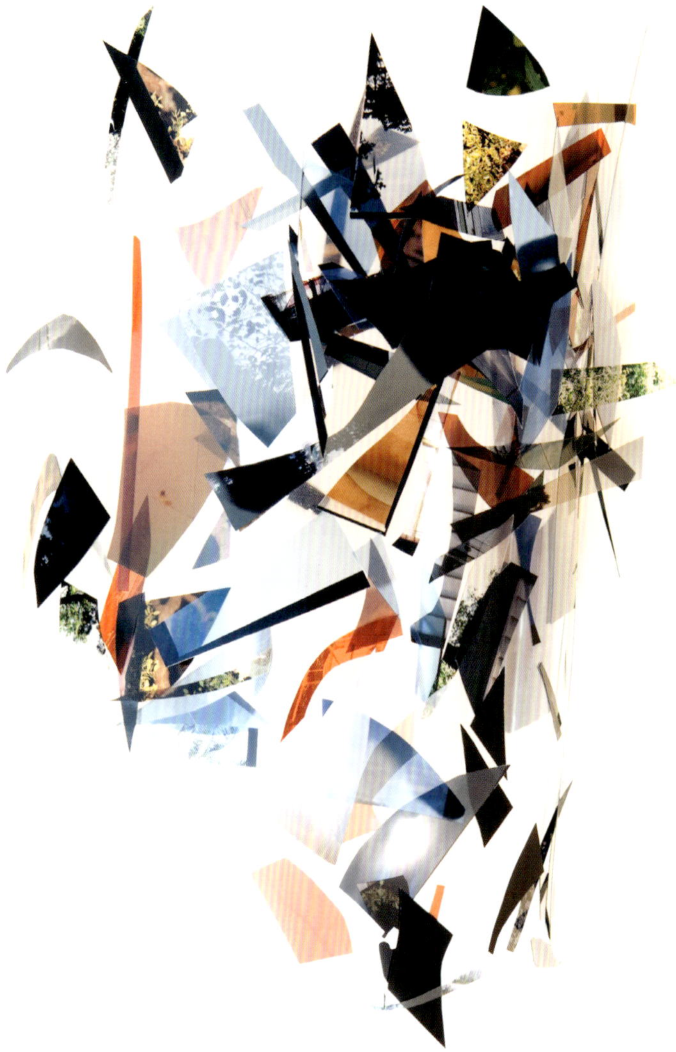

Brea Souders, *Film Electric #9*, 2012
archival inkjet print (dimensions variable)
Courtesy of the artist and Bruce Silverstein Gallery, NY

Working with randomly gathered "film piles", Brea Souders creates defined photo assemblages using castaway negatives: shards of footage, live motion terminally reassigned to stasis—at least in the dimensional sense. As a framed photograph, *Film Electric #9*, 2012, remains charged and dynamic, frenetic even. Charged psychically as a personal anthology—impressionist memories linked by chance, an esoteric testimony for our viewing pleasure. And charged materially, too, a result of the artist's creative process.

> I scatter pieces of film that I've cut up over larger pieces of acetate that I cut into various shapes.... The acetate is rubbed against a hard surface to create a static cling. Then I lift the sheets up to hang against a wall and photograph it. Pieces of film fall to the ground, and the remaining pieces will sometimes rearrange themselves—some pieces are attracted to one another while others are repelled.[1]

From the din of collective memory, new associations are made.

The outcome works as a striking metaphor for the storage and retrieval of personal information: in their construction—enacting the very process of memory and time, sorting through interior history; and in their actualization—angled, fragmented scenes. While not whole, they are not unformed. *Film Electric #9* is consolidated and yet, discrete. The facts are chopped but they are solid, providing anchors from which to hold our focus.

We are splintered organisms, with creased paths that bridge and turn on themselves. Our patterns repeat but our surroundings and affiliations hover in constant flux. Like *Film Electric #9*, we too exist in multiple states, as discrete particles that each point to their own eventuality and convergence.

Each piece is simultaneously essential and irrelevant to the totality. Remove a shard and everything changes, yet the piece remains extant. We bestow importance onto each colour, each transparency, each visual palimpsest, the size, the placement, even the voids—searching for clues in the absence of any linear narrative.

Film Electric #9 doesn't want to tell us much, but I want to ask. What came before (I see yellow grass; I see green grass), what could have been (I don't see hands); and what refuse instead chose to linger, enacting and rupturing the artist's history (and what refuse succumbed, falling to the periphery)? Is this Souders's most forthright portrait, the most 'natural' in its totality?

Souders makes effective (and affective) use of negative space. Her framing evokes the unconscious, lost memories, pictures never taken. Does the absence itself perform? If harmony is a simultaneous combination of tones, there is also harmony to this perceived absence (which is itself, present) and a harmony to Souders's implied chaos. Honouring both the void and the anarchic, this fragmentary 'portrait' gloriously nods to the mundane.

Fragments exist on their own, but not really. A fragment could not be a fragment without that which is lacking. The fragments here are our cryptic raconteurs. They are the viewer's tour guides, presenting an intentionally disjointed history by means of a fractured dialogue, an indeterminate dialogue. Linkages transposed, connected by experience and sensory memories: light, texture, colour, shape; a hand that isn't there.

We are an observer of the whole, while Souders, in her process, is an observer of the parts. We may interpret, yet the assemblages dismiss definitive conclusion.

Arianne Di Nardo

1. Di Nardo, Arianne, "A Conversation with Brea Souders", *Lavalette*, 2013. Accessed 14 May 2015 http://www.lavalette.com/a-conversation-with-brea-souders/

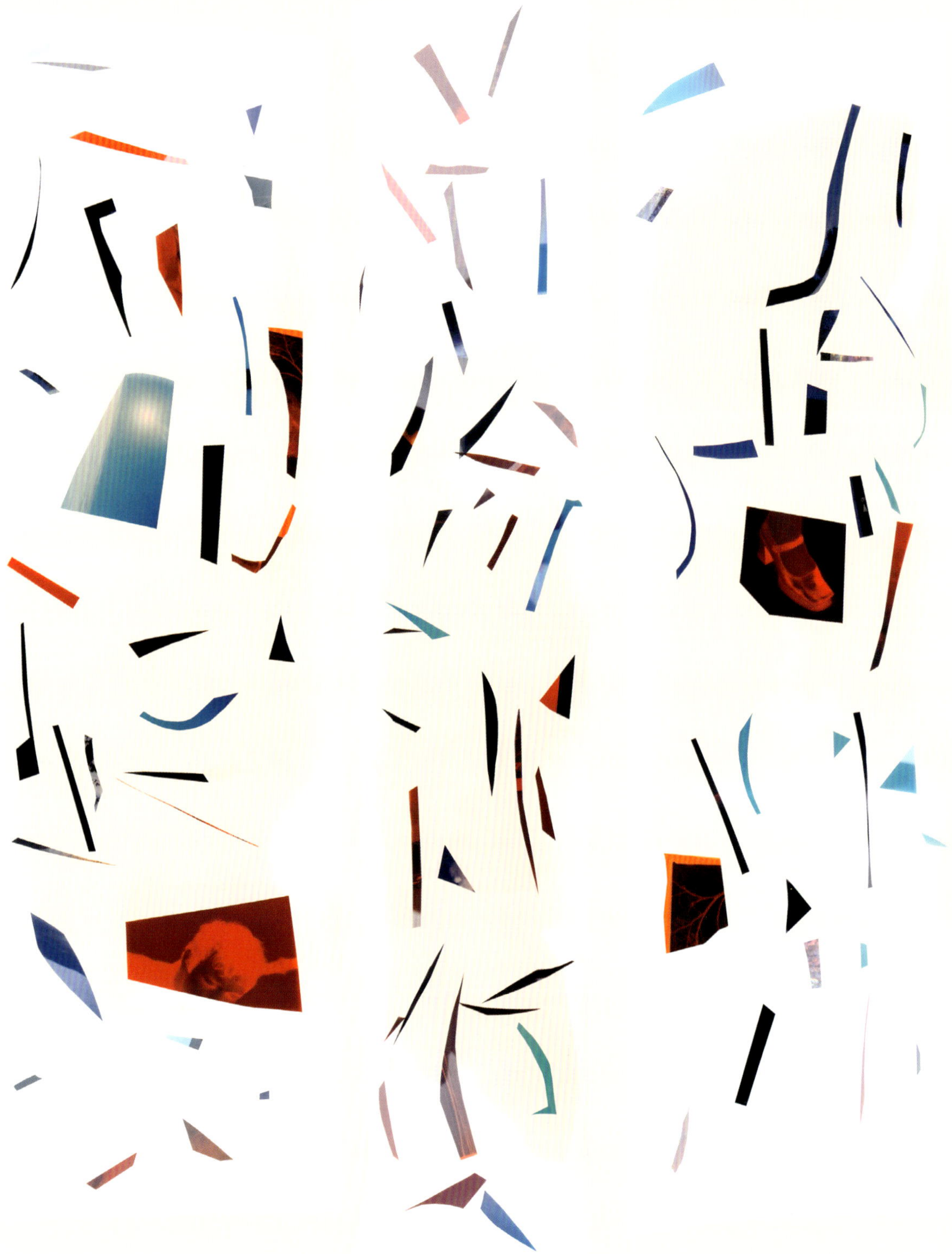

Brea Souders, *Film Electric #4*, 2012
archival inkjet print (dimensions variable)
Courtesy of the artist and Bruce Silverstein Gallery, NY

Walk into a hall of mirrors with your eyes closed. The mirrors will reflect, but the internal reflex of your eyes will remain dark. Ever ready but not activated by light. Things past the protection of your eyelids race back and forth. All things past your eyelids that are there, are there. They are real. And inside, your eyes are waiting.

Squeeze your eyes tight as you can and what comes. Colour. Shapes. Facsimiles of what you are used to perceiving. Things that are hidden from the world. Fragments that light forgot. They only exist inside. They seem jumbled. Elusive. And at the same time they are highly related and fixed in their right place. Like cousins thrown in a bathtub after an annual family picnic.

You must realize. These are not your cousins and there is no bathtub. And though the facsimiles are actually originals, they sustain themselves and come from a place you get to by opening your eyes. They are much like memory, like a feint of some larger biology. They are where you rejuvenate. And they are where your worry goes when it goes away. Open your eyes.

Now you inquire. What does a steady hand wrapped firmly around the small of your neck feel like. Like the start of remorse. Of romance. Of confusion. Of submission. Of diversion. What does it feel like when you believe you are the only person to feel a certain feeling. Or conversely, what is it like when you have the inkling that you might not be alone in it. That someone else may see things as you do. That your perceptions aren't an isolation, but a connection.

Questions beget questions. When you fall what happens. Do you break into a hundred pieces of colour? That is a moment beyond unity, beyond duality, beyond a tripartite, beyond some usual understanding of yourself and your surroundings. In that moment there is multiplicity and the voluminous detail of experience. Do you miss it? How did you find out? Why did you let that happen? Measure it out in handfuls. The measuring cups are the size of handfuls.

Uncertainties require certainties. It is natural to distrust what is confusing. To reject what you don't know. Somewhere in the reflections of light you will find your vanity and be comforted by it. You know who you are. You tell stories about yourself. You know yourself better the more you tell the stories. You create yourself. You are the creator.

Close your eyes again. Then open them just enough to see but so that from the outside they appear closed. There is tension at the edges of your eyelids. Your lips pucker slightly in disservice to your deception. Your brow is tight. With your eyes barely open you are engaged in an act of deprivation. The hall of mirrors is full of deprivation. You might go astray. But if you do not you will not be deprived.

Ray Gilliar

PROCESS

Annie MacDonell
and Alexis Dirks
Sophie Hackett
Sam Cotter
Sara Knelman
Sarah Robayo Sheridan
Sky Goodden
Saelan Twerdy
Kimberly Phillips
Natasha Chaykowski

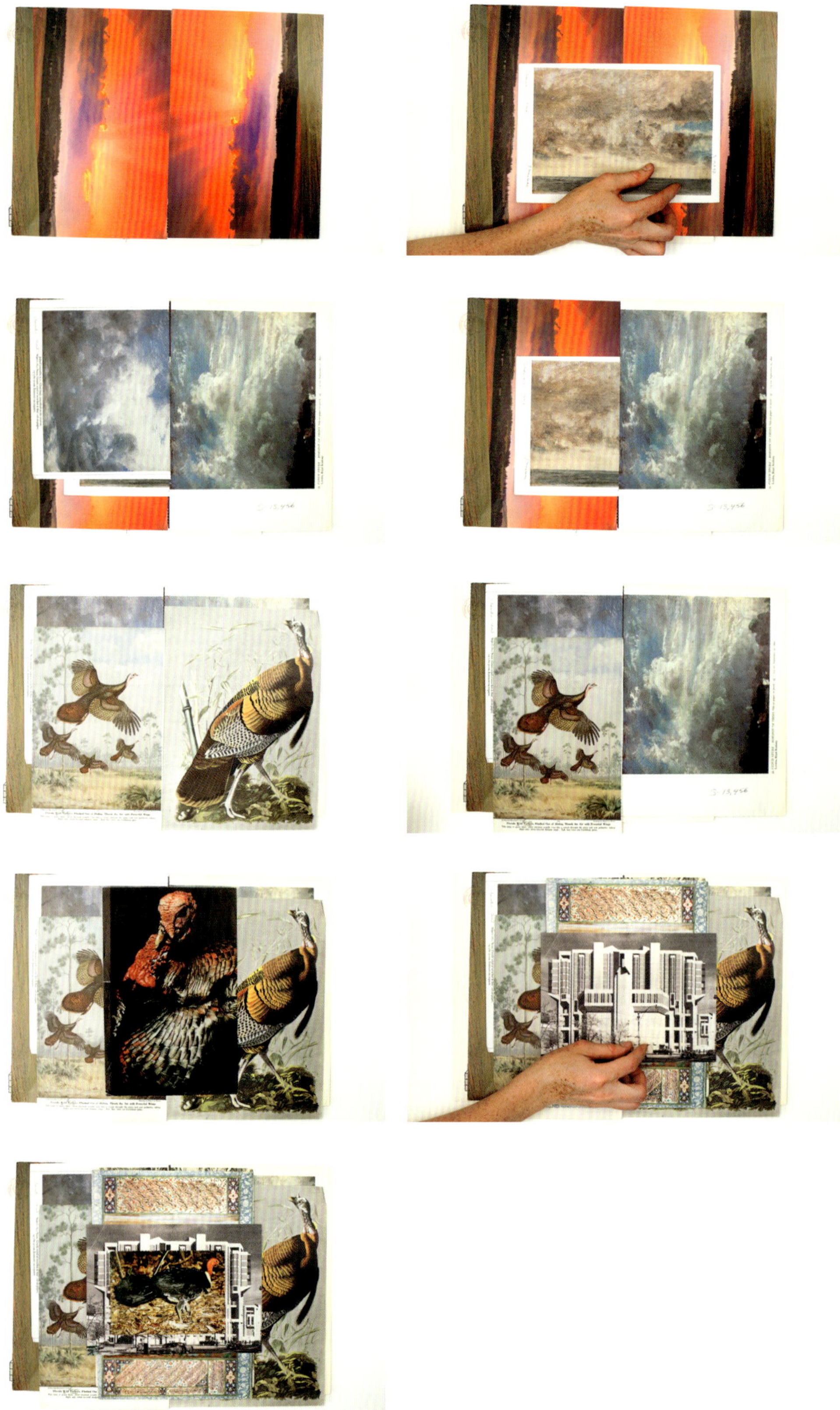

Annie MacDonell, documentation of the performance piece *The Bird and the Cup*, produced in collaboration with Maïder Fortuné, in May of 2014. Commissioned by the Scotiabank CONTACT Photography Festival
Photographs by Claire Harvie
Courtesy of the artist

Annie invites us to gather on the fifth floor of the Toronto Reference Library on the afternoon of 31 May, 2014. We sit in rows, parallel to a screen and to the left. Light streams through the windows behind, where bird shapes are attached to the glass. (Our avian friends are all around.) We wait, until she and her collaborator—French artist Maïder Fortuné—begin their lecture performance.

They sit at two tables. We watch as their hands delicately place pages, images, on an overhead projector. We see this unfold in front of us but also from above, on the screen.

Annie has spent hours, years, leafing through the filing cabinets that house the library's Picture Collection, more than a million images sorted into 32,000 subject categories, straightforward as well as strange. Though there is a system, its logic can only be described as idiosyncratic. The images on the projector are these, released from their folders, to build the tale of *The Bird and the Cup*, 2014.

The artists work with these images in a deliberate, business-like manner. They layer them, build stacks of them. They create new images in the process. The rasp and crinkle of paper follows, as they sift and move. They also take turns relaying the tale—something of a parable—describing it in clear, almost dispassionate, voices: two libraries, two women and a bird. We are transported.

Annie has contemplated the relationship between common space and individual thought, between architecture and knowledge. What does a room stand for? What ideas does it encourage? Do we best make stories together, alone or alone together?

> *The fundamental principle of design is described by the architect as the empty cup.... We tend to focus on the cup itself, its material, its form, its colour and pattern often forgetting that the essence of the cup is the emptiness inside it. Without the need for this emptiness there is no need for the cup.*

The artists created the lecture in the reference library. They watched people in the space, using the space, what they looked at, which stairs they took. Annie also told me she had been reading Frances Stark's *The Architect & The Housewife*. In the lecture performance, they contrast instead a librarian and a security guard, a keeper of knowledge and a keeper of space, doing their jobs, confronting their selves and their tasks.

> *But it is the vastness of the space that fills you with resolve, with intent, with determination. It is the roundness of its contours that incurs in you a sense of your own potentiality. It is the quality of the light, seeming to come from everywhere and nowhere all at once, that makes you feel that a divine experience is within your grasp. It is a void that you are experiencing, but this void is not a lack. The void is a space of limitless potential.*

The artists turn the images into birds. They take flight in our minds through the actions of the artists and the sounds of their voices. We are inside and we are outside. We can touch them. These are not metaphors.

We emerge onto the street, into a bright afternoon, as bright as the light the artists had described. I feel quiet. Dreamy. I have surrendered thought and feel instead the sun on my skin, sweat beginning to rise to its surface.

Sophie Hackett

Italicized text is from Annie MacDonell's performance, *The Bird and the Cup*, produced in collaboration with Maïder Fortuné, in May of 2014.

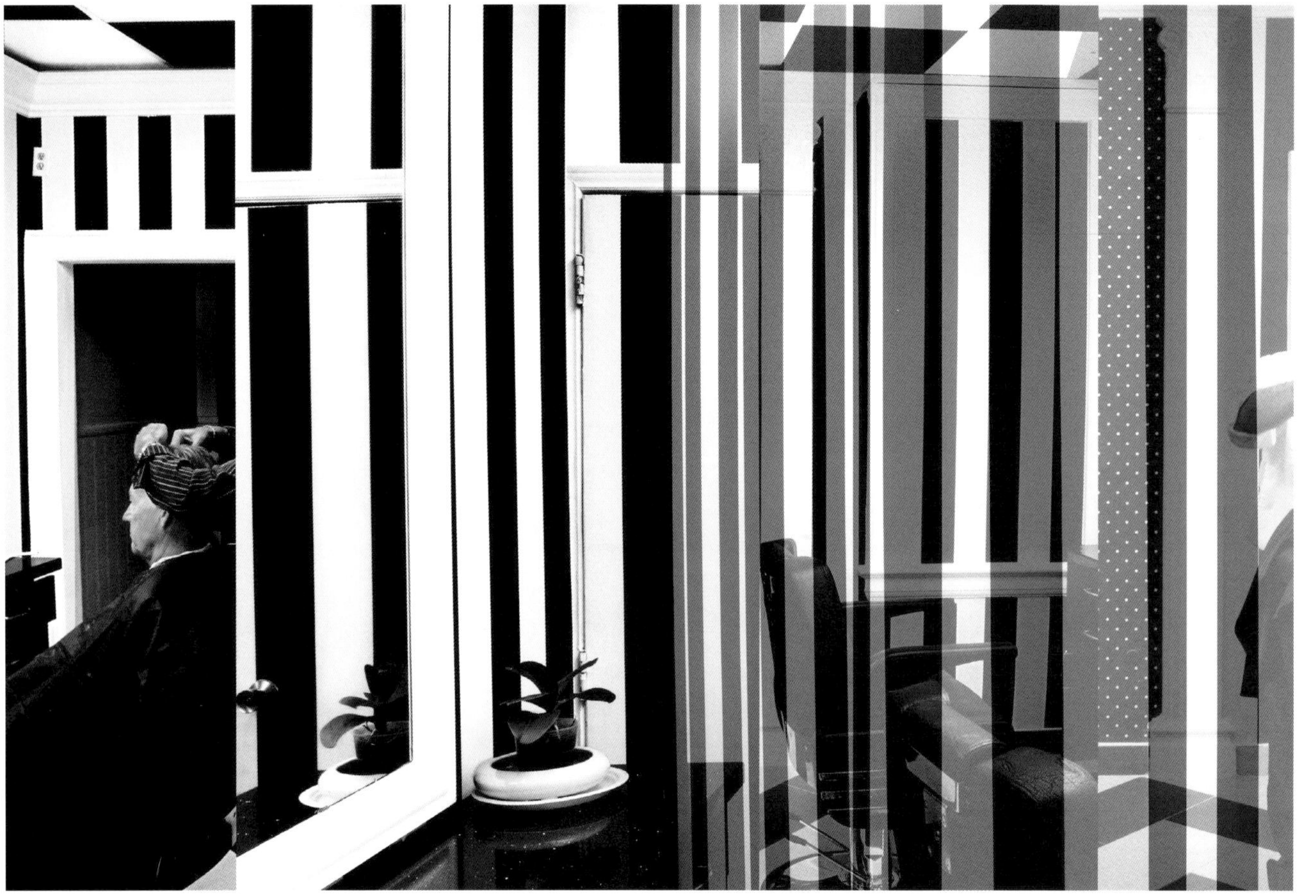

Annie MacDonell, *Untitled*, 2013
from the series *Flatness, Light, Black & White*,
18 x 12 inch inkjet print
Courtesy of the artist and Katharine Mulherin
Contemporary Art Projects

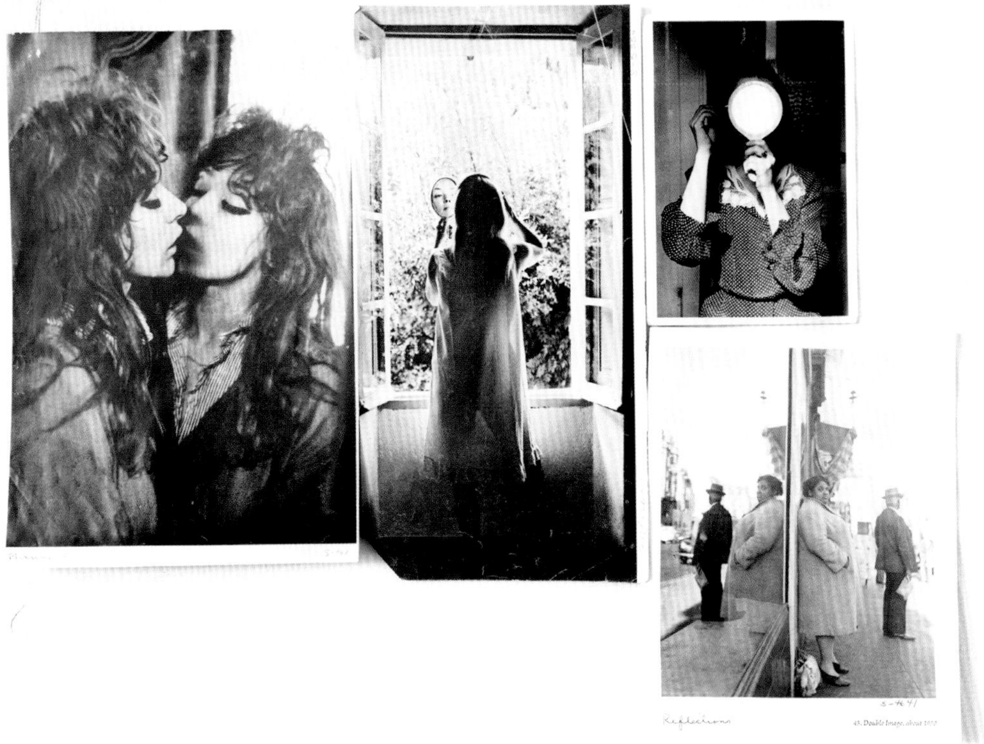

Annie MacDonell, *Untitled,* 2012
from the series *The Picture Collection,*
30 x 22 inch inkjet prints
Courtesy of the artist and Katharine Mulherin
Contemporary Art Projects

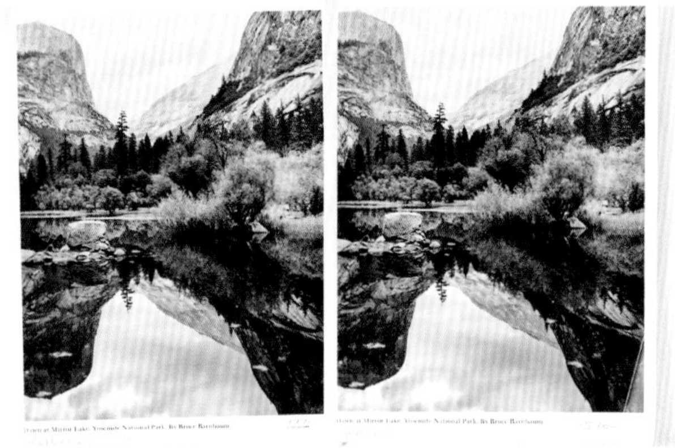

Annie MacDonell, *Untitled*, 2012
from the series *The Picture Collection*,
30 x 22 inch inkjet prints
Courtesy of the artist and Katharine Mulherin
Contemporary Art Projects

Images end time, existing outside it. Excerpted fragments of the past in the present. Cut off and closed forever: sitting in the archive, static on the studio wall. Their meanings finite, fixed and firm. The signs have been frozen and their possibilities charted. Arresting time, arresting space: a codex of arrested images. Signifier and signified becoming one.

The studio, the gallery, the eye of the storm: a meditative space. Classifying something as a "reflection" is a metaphysical act; malleability emerges yet two copies of the same image land in the same place. The logic of the past has a foothold in the present, so can there be any difference in the future? The forgotten distance between intention and interpretation.

The artist is a code breaker, breaking the images open to imbue them with other codes. Codes of her own design, dissecting the logic preceding her: academics, archivists and avant-gardes. The image is removed from the archive, it becomes unclassified, uncaptioned. It has been excerpted, taken from a continuum, declassified, recaptured, reframed. Looked at and looking, the rules have changed. The image has become something strange, an invocation in its presentation, still it remains the same.

In the archive she finds the same image twice. One image twice while also being two. Depth removed from the picture plane. Planar vision. But it is hard to see just one image, depth is replaced with complexity, giving way to a conceptual depth, not an optical one. The illusion of being different, yet all images are the same.

Images have life, extending into the future, through the past. Opening up, each one existing in many places at once. Circulating through parallel pasts and parallel presents. Here we can begin to take hold of them, not so much altering signs as exploring their possibilities, potentialities. Travelling through time, through space, through images. Signifier and signified exchanging places.

The archive, the artist, the eye of the viewer: a mediated space. Classifying something a "mirror" is a literal act, but things can be in two places at once. Photographs are always in many places at once, one foot rooted in the past the other firmly in the present. But there's also the future and all the forgotten distances between the past and present.

The artist is a time traveller, a voyager, ricocheting through a continuum, one of her own device governed by a logic preceding her. An image exists in an archive, codified, captioned. It has been excerpted, taken from a continuum, classified and framed. Framed again. Looked at and looking, the rules have changed, the image remains the same. Excavation but not preservation. Repetition and copy, emphasis and example. The parts are interchangeable, still it remains the same.

In a stereo card we see the same image twice. The same image twice with the illusion of being one, with depth inserted into the picture plane. Binocular vision. Here we see the same image twice, but the repetition removes optical depth giving us contextual depth. The illusion of being different, yet they are different.

Sam Cotter

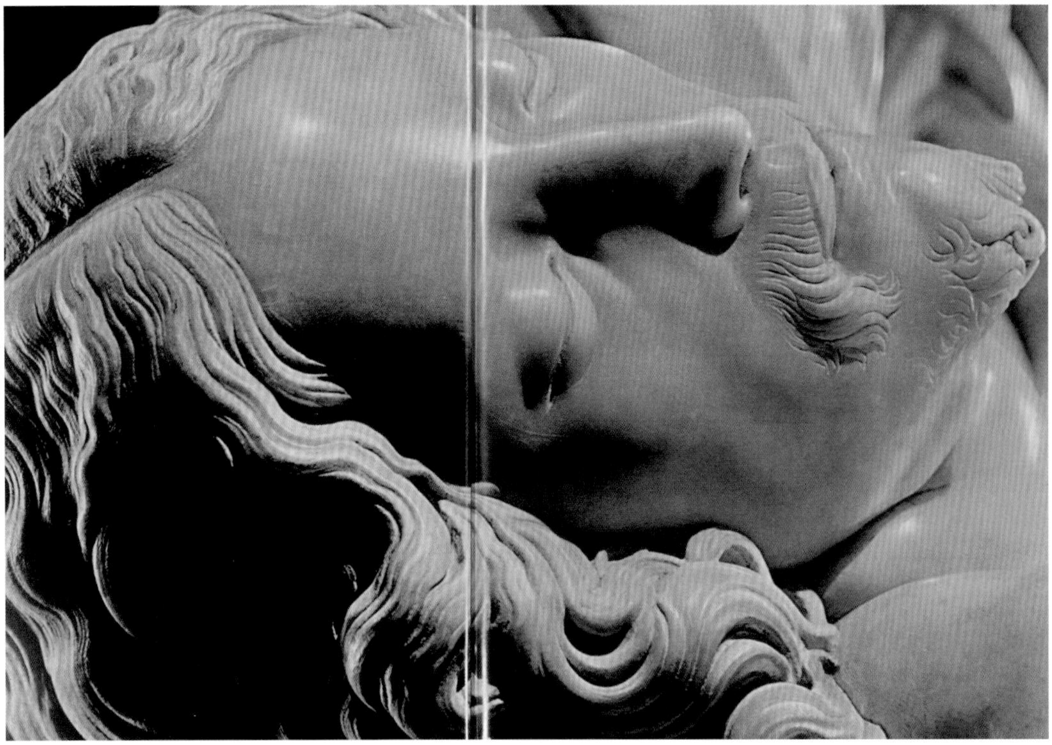

ON IMAGES OF IMAGES OF IMAGES

On sculpture[1]

On photographs of sculpture[2]

(On photographs of people posed after sculpture[3]

On photographs of photographs of people posed after sculpture[4])

On books of photographs of sculpture[5]

On slides of images in books of photographs of sculpture[6]

(On books of images of slides, including photographs of photographs and photographs of sculpture[7])

(On slideshows of images of sculpture and other arts, of family life and travel and everything else[8])

On digital scans of slides of images in books and magazines of photographs of sculpture[9]

On catalogue essays on digital scans of slides of images in books and magazines of photographs of sculpture.[10]

Annie MacDonell, found image, originally 35mm slide, scanned and uploaded to the internet as part of *Split Screen*, an online slideshow commissioned for eitherand.org project
Courtesy of the artist

1. *He has left it in many forms, sketches, half-finished designs, finished and unfinished groups of sculpture; but always as a hopeless, rayless, almost heathen sorrow—no divine sorrow, but mere pity and awe at the stiff limbs and colourless lips.*

2. *Everyone will have noticed how much easier it is to get hold of a picture, more particularly a piece of sculpture, not to mention architecture, in a photograph than in reality.*

3. *It is, of course, the stylized perfection of Praxiteles' or Phidias' marble nudes that we see in Neil's living torso: the flesh made art as much as the three dimensions of the body have been transformed into two.*

4. *The desire of representation exists only insofar as it can never be fulfilled, insofar as the original always is deferred.*

5. *An earlier generation thrived on Michelangelo; now we are given photographs of lesser masters, likewise of folk paintings and art hitherto ignored: in fact everything that comes into line with what we call a style is now being photographed.*

6. *More likely, you'll be using slides shot by a number of photographers, each with a different level of know-how and experience and a highly personal photographic style. And you—and your audiences—will see the differences, almost as easily as spotting the differences in a page of signatures.*

7. *A Persistent Blue Glow; Abstract Weather Patterns; Clouds in Grey Landscape; Chairs Missing; Stunt Doubles; Triple Shadows; Airports and Airports and Airplanes; From Gutters to Pagebreaks: A History; Central Motif: Performance Stills, Installation Shots, and Canadian Landscapes; Single Double Double Triple Quadruple.*

8. *Borrowed from the realm of souvenir hunting—where they allowed travelers to collect and hoard their memories, and families to archive the major and minor events of their lives—they rapidly overtook black-and-white glossies and more costly photo transparencies to become the primary means by which images traveled from studio to gallery and curatorial offices, and from there to seminar rooms and lecture halls.*

9. *But the spine's interruption of the image reminds us of where they came from in the first place, and how our ways of encountering them continue to shift along with the technology that delivers them to us.*

10. See Benjamin, Walter, "A Small History of Photography", 1931, in Edmund Jephcott and Kingsley Shorter, trans, *One-Way Street and Other Writings*, London: NLB, 1979, pp 240–257; Barb Choit, *Ten Shows*, London/Vancouver: Black Dog/Or Gallery, 2014; Crimp, Douglas, "The Photographic Activity of Postmodernism", in *On the Museum's Ruins*, Mass: The MIT Press, 1993, pp 108–125; Kenny, Michael F and Raymond F Schmitt, *Images, Images, Images: The Book of Programmed Multi-Image Production*, New York: Eastman Kodak Company, 1983; MacDonell, Annie, "Split Screen", http://eitherand.org/eitherand/split-screen/; Malraux, André, "Museum Without Walls", in Stuart Gilbert, trans, *The Voices of Silence*, London: Secker and Warburg, 1954, pp 13–128; Pater, Walter, "The Poetry of Michelangelo", in *The Renaissance: Studies in Art and Poetry*, Berkeley and Los Angeles: University of California Press, 1980 [1893], pp 57–76; Solomon-Godeau, Abigail, "Winning the Game When the Rules Have Been Changed: Art Photography and Postmodernism", *Screen*, 25 (6), 1984, pp 88–103; Storr, Robert, "Next Slide, Please..." in Darsie Alexander, ed, *SlideShow*, Baltimore: The Baltimore Museum of Art, 2005, pp 51–69.

Sara Knelman

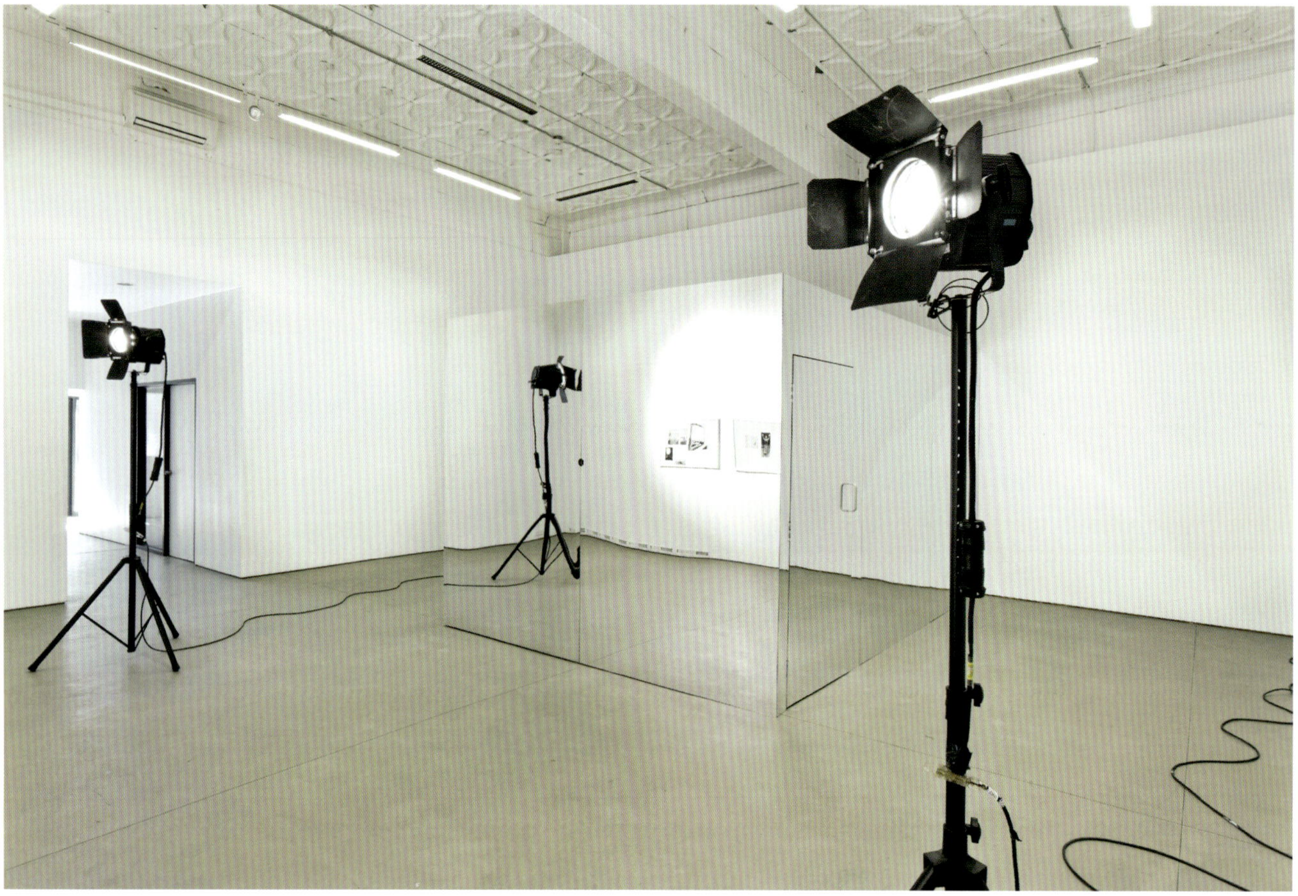

Annie MacDonell, installation view of the exhibition "Originality and the Avant Garde (on art and repetition)", five photographs, lights, and a free-standing mirrored structure serving both as projection booth and camera obscura (dimensions variable), Mercer Union, Toronto, 2012
Photograph by Toni Hafkenscheid
Courtesy of the artist

While working at Mercer Union, I was privileged to witness this artwork's unfurling from concepts spoken to ideas committed into physical being. The invitation was offered, according to the centre's ethos, as a flexible platform in which variance was a welcome prospect. Indeed, MacDonell's realization exceeded the ambition of the proposal. The exhibition's title "Originality and the Avant Garde (on art and repetition)" signalled the circle of quotation that circumscribed her project. Emphasizing principles at the core of photography—duplication, reversal, adaptation, and mimesis—MacDonell staged an exhaustive set of repetitions springing from found print media clippings, in turn arranged into clusters photographed and framed, the series inverted in an image revealed by a mirror-clad camera obscura that reflected the contents of the room and which also doubled as a black box cinema to project a video copy of a 16mm film. The video repeated the images loaned from the "mirror" and "reflection" files of the Toronto Reference Library's Picture Collection, adding a repetitious monologue and voiceover. The video's looped projection paused in alternation with the faint camera obscura image whose slow reveal straddled the cusp of discernability. Studio lights directed at the photographs mounted to the gallery wall aided the registration of an image in the camera obscura but also formally announced the transposition between the studio and the gallery. As a further illustration of the theme of origin and derivative, the dimensions of the artist's studio (a room in her home), were mapped onto the camera obscura's construction. By positing an equivalency between production and display, MacDonell invoked contemporary image mechanics in which capture and transmission is a near simultaneous process. Drawing from the archive at the Toronto Reference Library allowed her to contrast the rapid-fire algorithmic shuffling of images online with the analogue precursor of a hand-assembled image bank and its somewhat idiosyncratic subject files. The images in that archive, loosened from their original editorial captions, seem to foresee the process of decontextualization that marks the trade in images today. In reviewing the image reproduced here, I understand that it is available to me as an indexical entry point to my lived experience of the exhibition. On the other hand, the documentation offers its own picture, not bounded by the context. One could see it as an added iteration in the process of image constitution and circulation. Here Toni Hafkenscheid's own framing aligns the meeting of the gallery wall and floor with the reflected image of the same in the mirrored cube. This specific effect corresponds to something that MacDonell's friend and fellow artist Chris Curreri remarked about his perception of the installation, which is that the surrogate version of the artist's studio appears to vanish into space, a physical boundary dissipated within the visual register. In this image we find but one possible representation within the many as yet catalogued interactions of light, time and lens, assuring us of a confirmed future for image-making in a time of image-saturation.

Sarah Robayo Sheridan

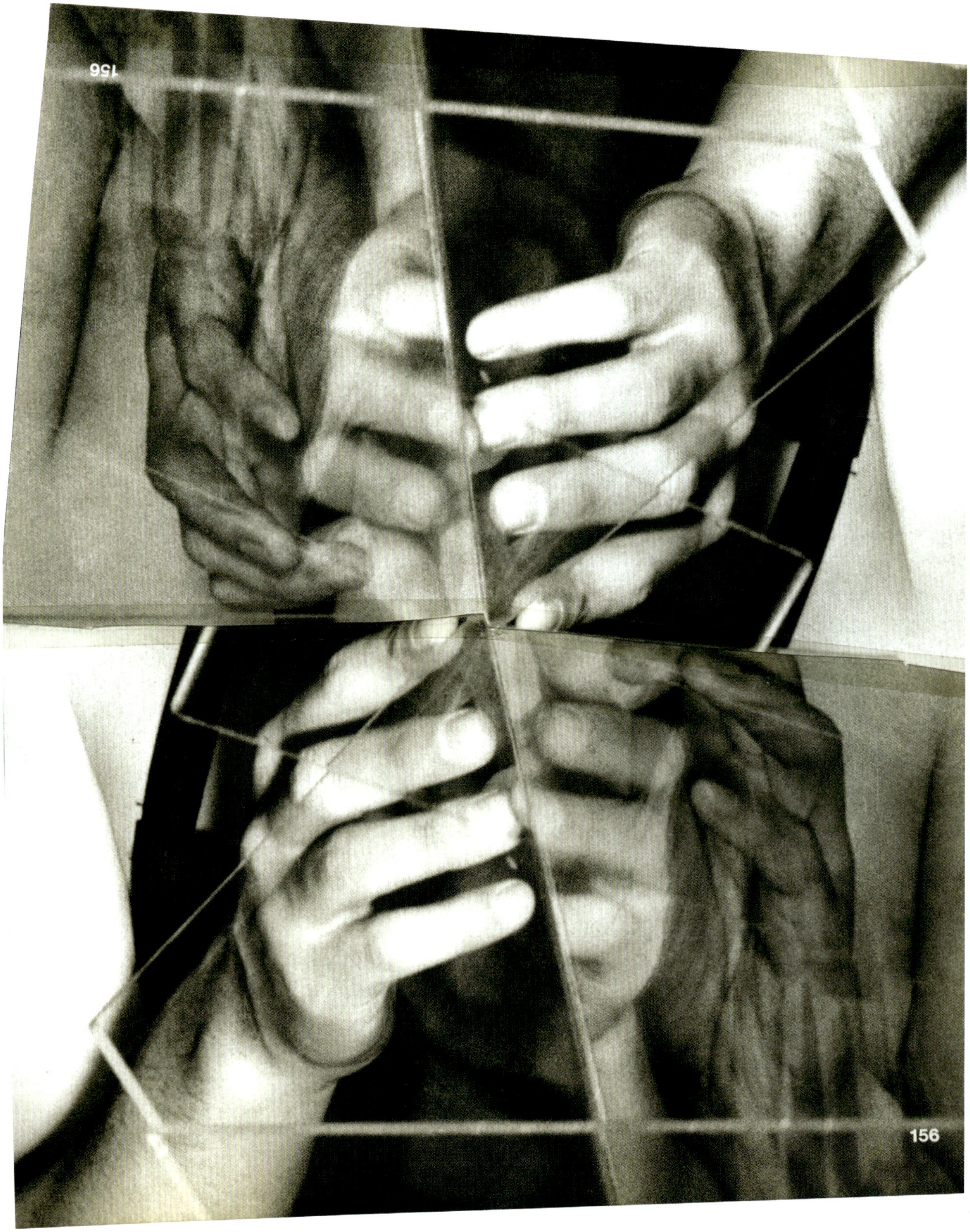

Annie MacDonell, *Untitled (Hand Collage)*, 2010
10 x 10 inch book pages and tape
Courtesy of the artist

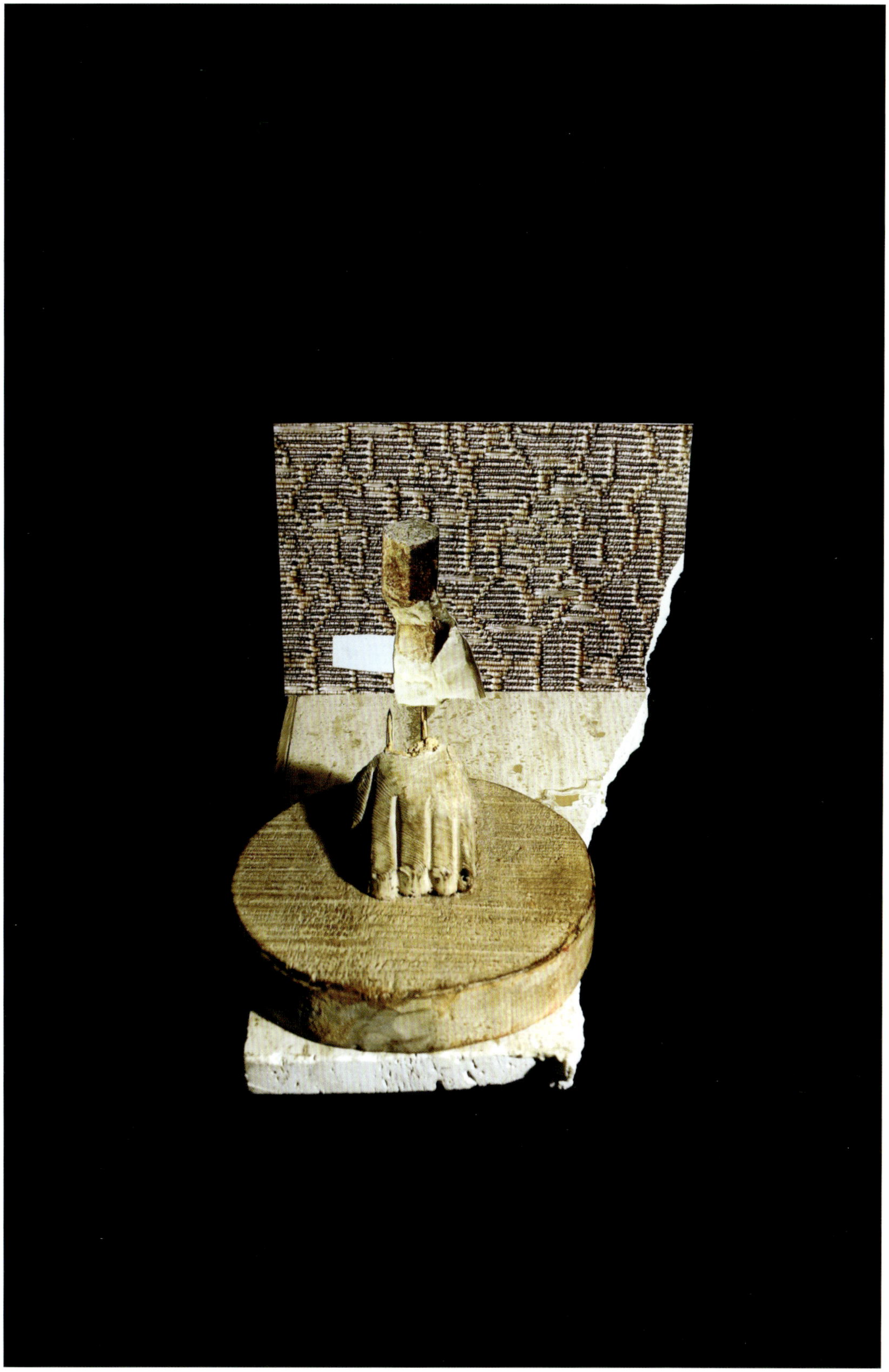

Alexis Dirks, *Keystone*, 2012
9 x 14 inch digital c-print
Courtesy of the artist

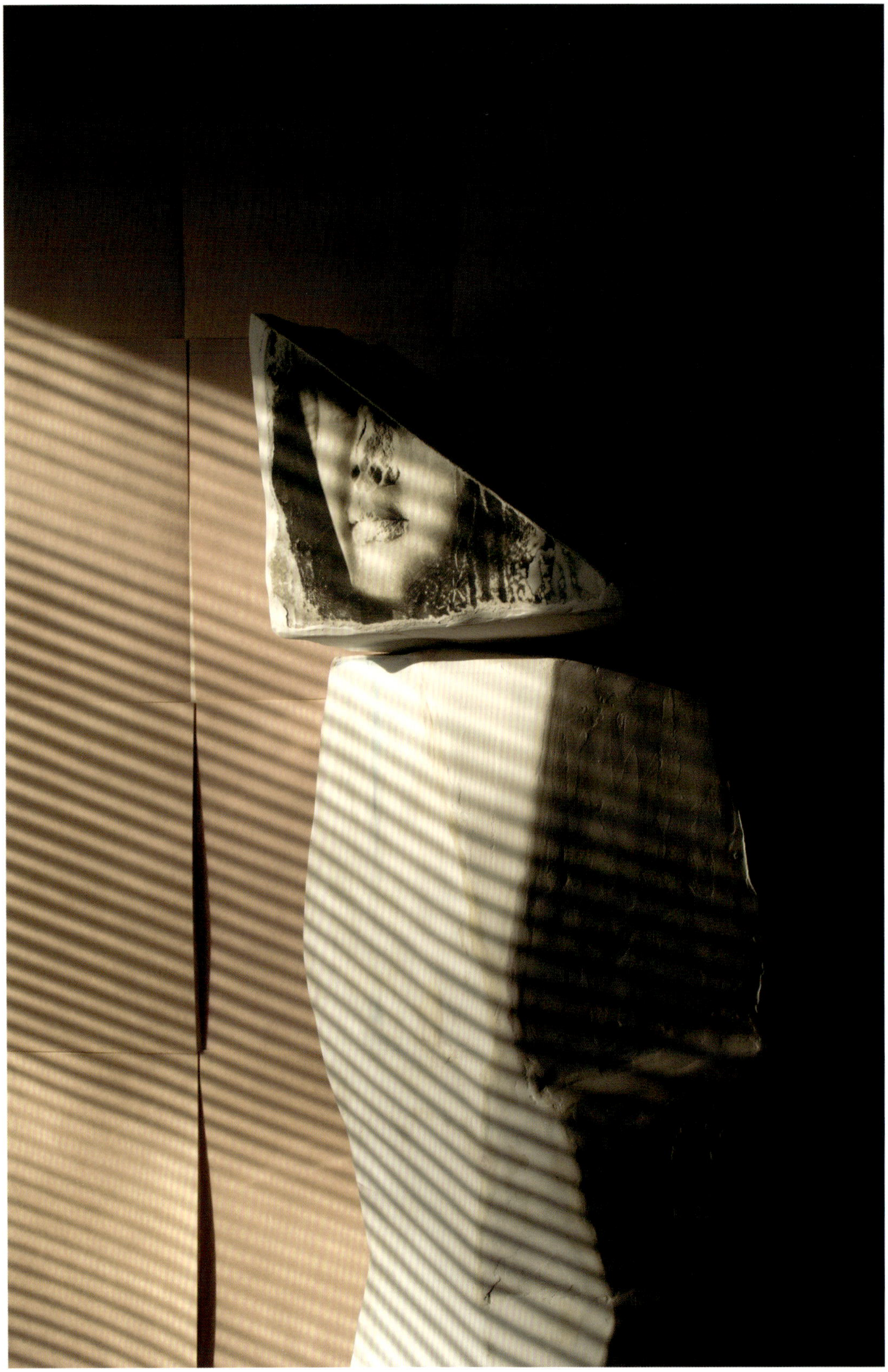

Alexis Dirks, *Blinds*, 2014
16 x 24 inch digital c-print
Courtesy of the artist

> The interior is not only the universe but also the *étui* of the private person. To live means to leave traces.... The detective story that follows these traces comes into being.
> Walter Benjamin[1]

Alexis Dirks is an artist of half-built memorials and dropped traces. Between fragment and fiction, monument and shadow, the artist directs our gaze beyond the "body we see"—whether plinth, rock, or picture—and invokes a history, an unsolved crime, a phantom memory. She produces correspondences that push beyond the limits of their media, and so we hunt an elusive protagonist. We pick at dropped threads, construct narrative to cover the seams, and eke out a story's conclusion, however much in vain. The bodies she plants form her recurring site, the place of stopped traces but still wringing for resolve.

Photography, as both the proof and preservation of disappearance, is central to Dirks's practice. *Missing Woman*, 2013, pins a cosmetic portrait between similarly-silenced pictures of moss-covered rocks and jutting crystal. Where Roland Barthes elucidated the essential quality of disappearance in photography, paradoxically positioning it within the very materiality of its subject (in *Camera Lucida*, he writes, "In the Photograph, the event is never transcended for the sake of something else: the Photograph always leads the corpus I need back to the body I see."[2]), Dirks continues to return us to the "body we see" as if to remind us that it is still missing, the image a mere receipt for presence. Something anecdotal, and disturbed.

The seeking that correspondence requires, the process of turning event to story: we wander through interiors with such assignments. The "*étui*", Walter Benjamin's paradigm for the casing in which we leave our quiet traces, is etched by memory and stories untold. "To live means to leave traces", he writes. "The detective story that follows these traces comes into being."[3]

Dirks marries media as old as time (geologic silhouettes) with fleeting light and shadow play. Between these—her form and spectre—Dirks leaves a trace of the briefest corporeal gesture: a hand, a face, a limb, something present that suggests something's missing. In *Blinds*, 2014, the eyes are gone; in *Missing Woman*, the girl. Dirks digs down under her photographic starting point and forms a haunted station. Holes feature strongly, as do paths that lead to unfinished profiles. We become her roper, the onsite agent to complete her fragmented project. We ask, "where else and what more?" We ask, "how now?", of the body we see.

Sky Goodden

1. Benjamin, Walter, "Paris, Capital of the Nineteenth Century, (Exposé of 1939)", *The Arcades Project*, Cambridge, MA: Belknap Press, 2002, p 20.
2. Barthes, Roland, *Camera Lucida*, New York: Hill and Wang, 1981, p 5.
3. Benjamin, "Paris, Capital of the Nineteenth Century, (Exposé of 1939)", p 20.

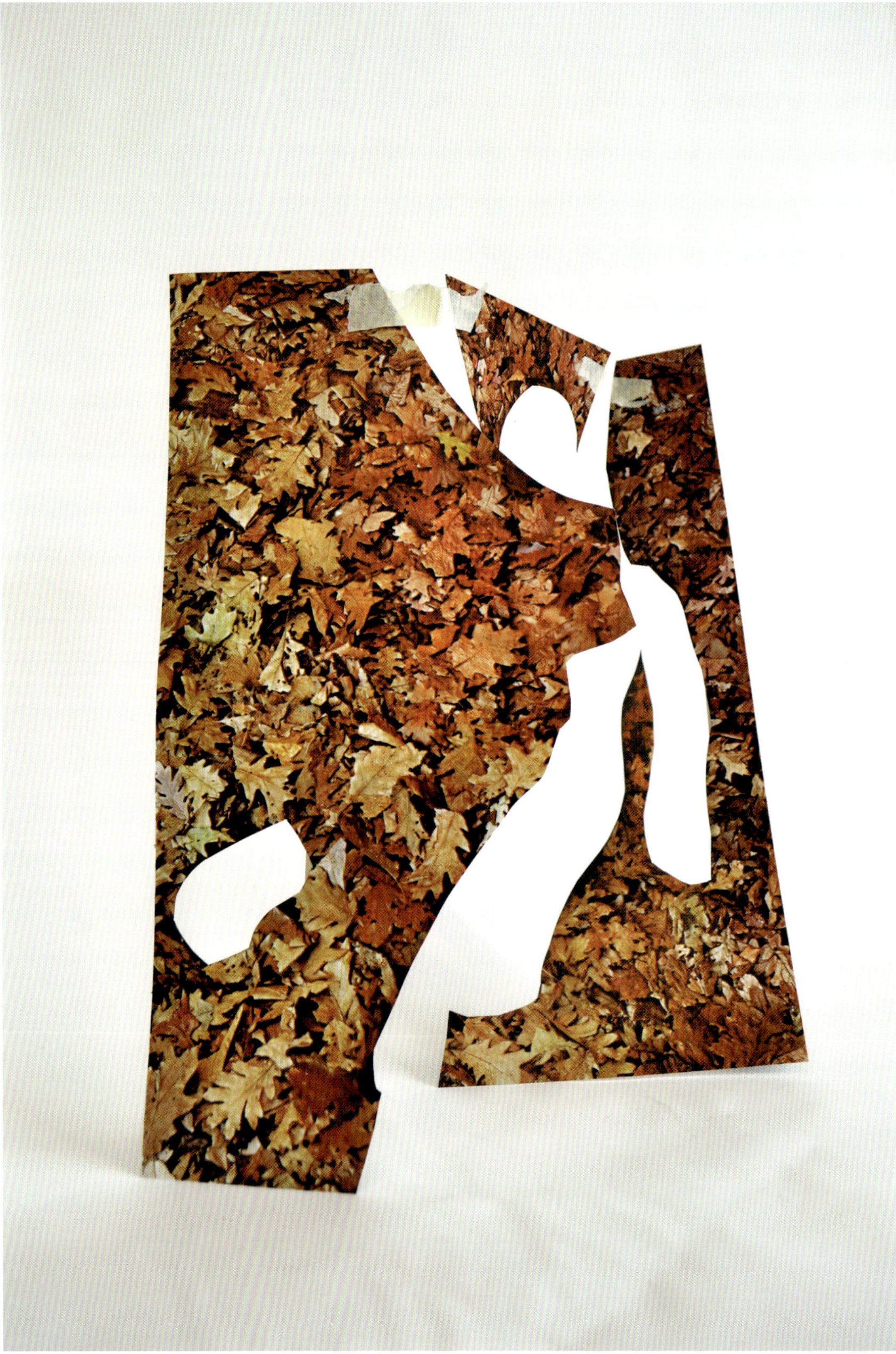

Alexis Dirks, *Missing Woman*, 2013
12 x 17 inch digital c-print
Courtesy of the artist

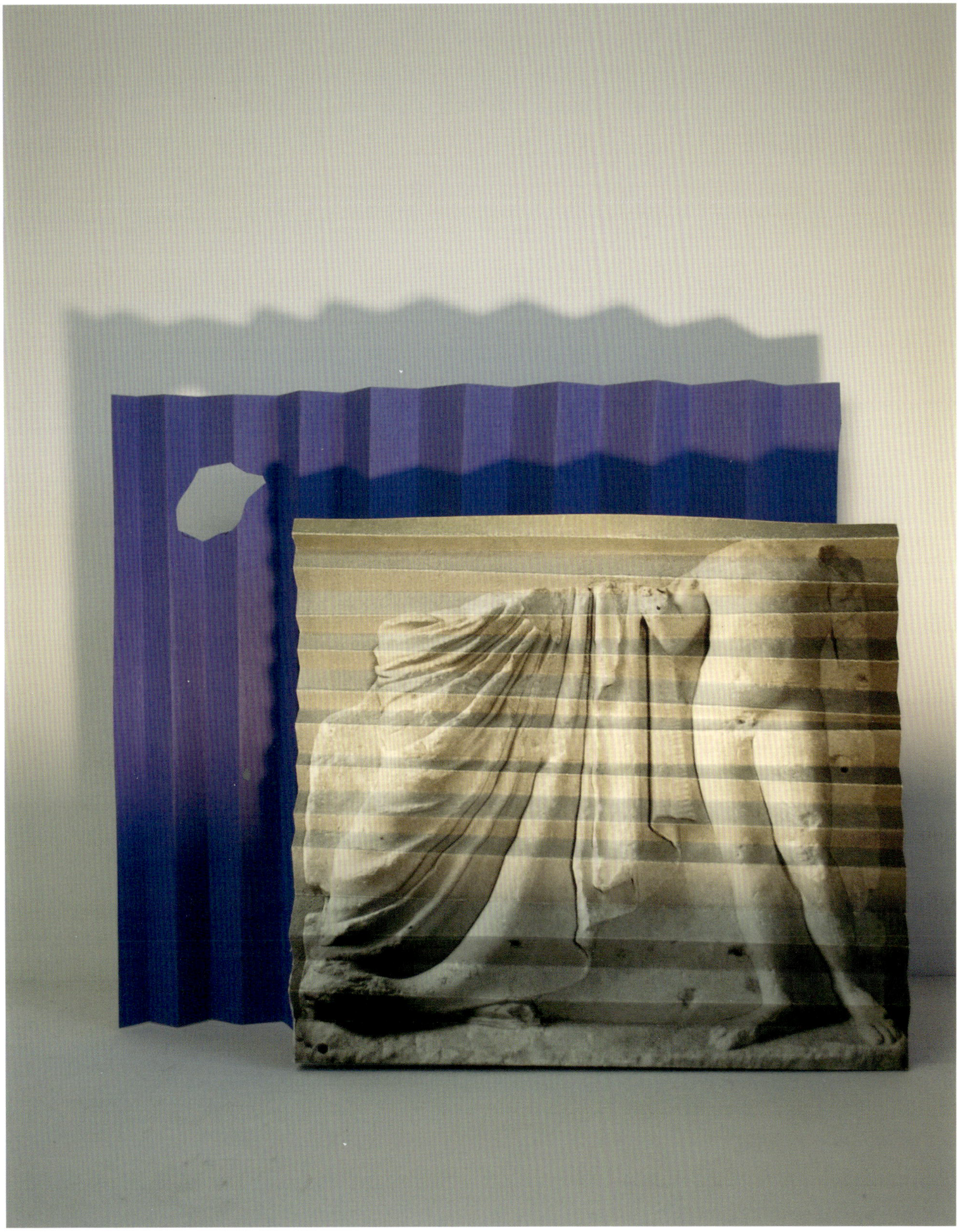

Alexis Dirks, *Folded Statue*, 2014
16 x 20 inch digital c-print
Courtesy of the artist

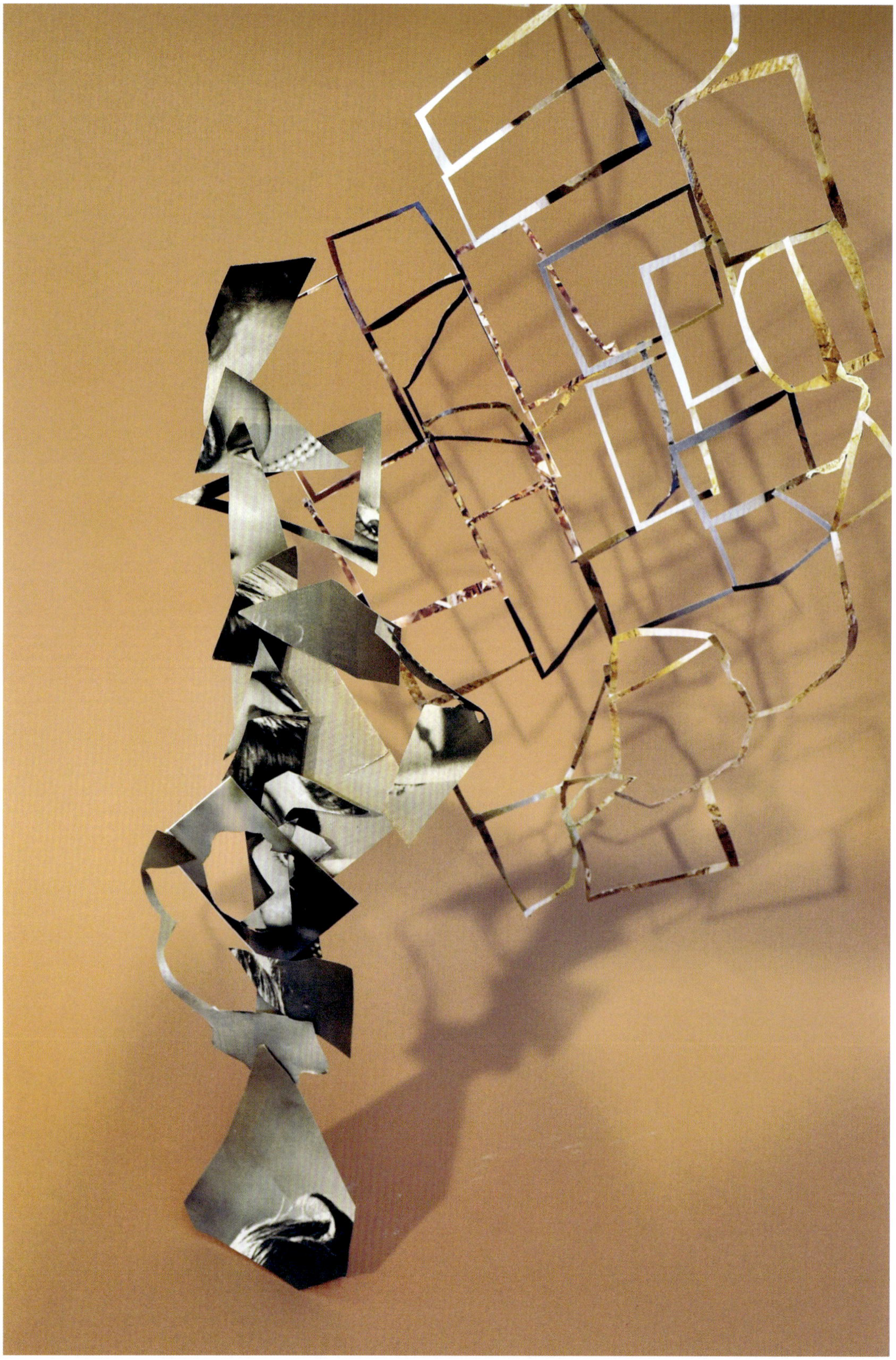

Alexis Dirks, *Net*, 2011
12 x 18 inch digital c-print
Courtesy of the artist

Alexis Dirks is all about the aesthetics of intrigue. Or maybe that is not right. Intrigue implies seduction, intimacy, plots and conspiracies that require at least two people to be in on the scheme. Intrigue implies a juicy story, but what Dirks is after, I think, is allure without a narrative. Her materials are almost always found photographs or objects, but rather than attempting to discover or create a backstory, she takes care to strip away as much as possible. She abstracts by creating uncertainty. When you are not sure what you are looking at, it is just a pure form: colour, texture, geometry, patina. The uncanny-valley curve she plays with is about how much information you can take away while still creating mystery, fascination, the desire to know. Subtract a little bit of context and you increase curiosity, but subtract too much and you pass into unintelligibility. Lose too much reference and you lose interest. It ceases to be a picture and just becomes nothing. But at the right point on the curve, you hit maximum allure.

In part, this explains why Dirks is more oriented to landscapes than portraits: faces, hairstyles, and clothes give away too many clues. They make things too definite. Figures, when they appear in her work, are usually statues, and often ones defeatured by time and wear, or abstract by design—a common, deliberate confusion in her images is about whether you are looking at something ancient or modern. Often, the figure/ground relation is thrown into question entirely: is it a rock formation, a fragment of architecture, a work of art? Is it floating in the air or lying on the ground? Is it flat, or does it have volume, extension, mass?

This preference for indeterminacy often leads Dirks towards non-human forms, like moss or timber, or even inorganic ones: rock, metal, cement, and rust, for instance. With these things, the question of provenance (when is it from, and where?) can occupy a much broader span. It can invoke geological time, in a way that a lot of minimal and earthwork sculpture did in the late 1960s and 70s.

Which is why this particular image is something of an anomaly, at least compared to her more recent work. It is clearly the kind of picture for which she cuts up found photos, builds them into a temporary sculpture, and then photographs it, but it is definitely a portrait. The totemic stack of black-and-white scraps on the left is clearly a woman. You can still detect fragments of her hair and pearl necklace, bathed in the perfume of vintage light. I am tempted to compare it to a mutilated Cindy Sherman *Untitled Film Still* (it is equally anonymous, reduced to an abstract trope of glamour rather than a specific person), but "mutilation" is the wrong word to describe the delicacy of Dirks's montage. The woman-figure seems to be dancing with a geometric cloud of razor-thin paper mesh in gemstone tones. It resembles a piece of jewelry that, like Dirks's source material, has passed through several states: personified, then abstracted. Taken together, their combined shadows swirl like a wisp of smoke. The photograph has all the earmarks of intrigue in its original sense. Two mysterious strangers meet on an empty dancefloor. Where did they come from? What did one whisper in the other's ear? We will never know.

Saelan Twerdy

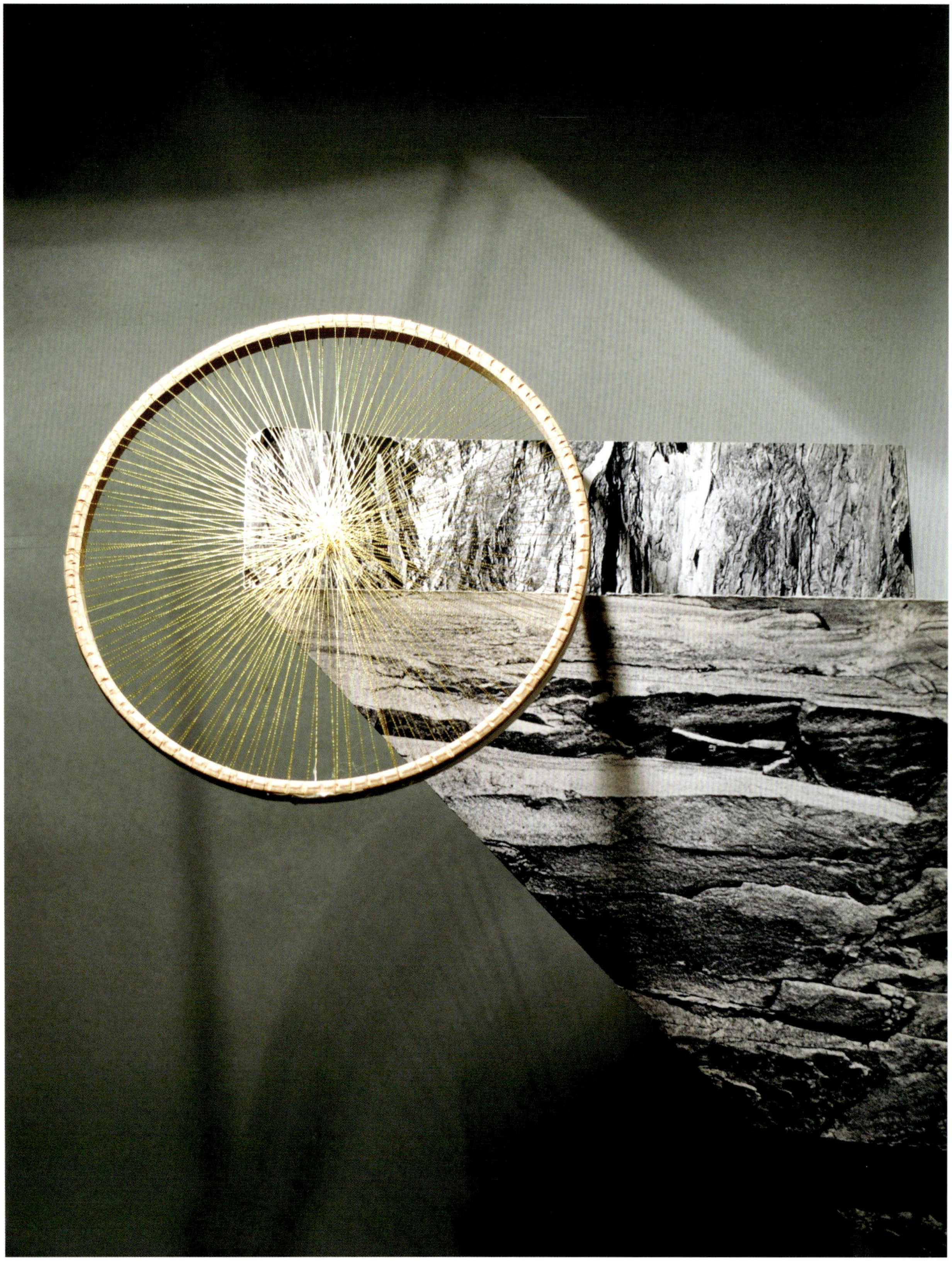

Alexis Dirks, *Mountain Threads*, 2011
15 x 19 inch digital c-print
Courtesy of the artist

> Things-in-themselves and things-as-they-are for us. Often by chance, [...] a simple object (a bobbin, a sampler, a scrap of lace) reveals itself here at the surface of the visible, by mystic documentary telepathy. Quickly. Precariously. Coming as it does from an opposite direction. If you are lucky, you may experience a moment before.[1]

My introduction to Alexis Dirks's *Mountain Threads* coincided, strangely, with another encounter: that of the verse of contemporary American poet Susan Howe. Like Dirks, Howe is "a haunter of archives". Her poetry, which wanders across theoretical and disciplinary boundaries, draws on historical documents and long-forgotten marginalia—scrawled notes, drawings, faded photographs, scraps of textiles. She weaves these materials into collage-poems that expose a porousness between the visual and the verbal, and between the past and our conjuring of it.

Howe speaks of the "telepathy of archives" (she defines telepathy as a feeling from afar), as though the archival materials themselves were capable of signalling, like semaphores, or reaching towards us across a vast distance, in some attempt to be understood.[2] It is at once the intimacy of this material—its tactility, its insistent presence—that is communicated in the texture of Howe's poetry (we are reminded that the English words *text* and *textile* are both drawn from the Latin *textere*, meaning "that which is woven") and the expanse of space between these messengers and ourselves.

Alexis Dirks also gathers materials from her surroundings, from that which is close at hand. Mined from the seemingly endless strata of things produced by and marooned within the world, it might be said that for Dirks, too, certain objects and images "speak", revealing themselves "at the surface of the visible". She edits, fragments and layers this selected ephemera, assembles it into sculptural installations—rendered as strange, textured landscapes, ambiguous in scale—and finally, photographs the sculptures, reassigning them to two-dimensionality. Hers is the shadowy, interior space of the half-remembered, the collectively felt; where things-as-they-are-to-us, to borrow Howe's vocabulary again, revert to things-in-themselves and are rendered distant: still recognizable but unreachable. What telepathy do Dirks's images practice? Across what distance do these relics speak?

*Relic: from the Latin relinquere, "to leave behind".

Kimberly Phillips

1. Howe, Susan, "The Whispered Rush, Telepathy of Archives", *Academy of American Poets Blaney Lecture*, New York: The New School, Friday, October 21, 2011. http://www.poets.org/poetsorg/text/video-blaney-lecture-whispered-rush-telepathy-archives.
2. See Howe, Susan, *Spontaneous Particulars: The Telepathy of Archives*, New York: New Directions, 2014.

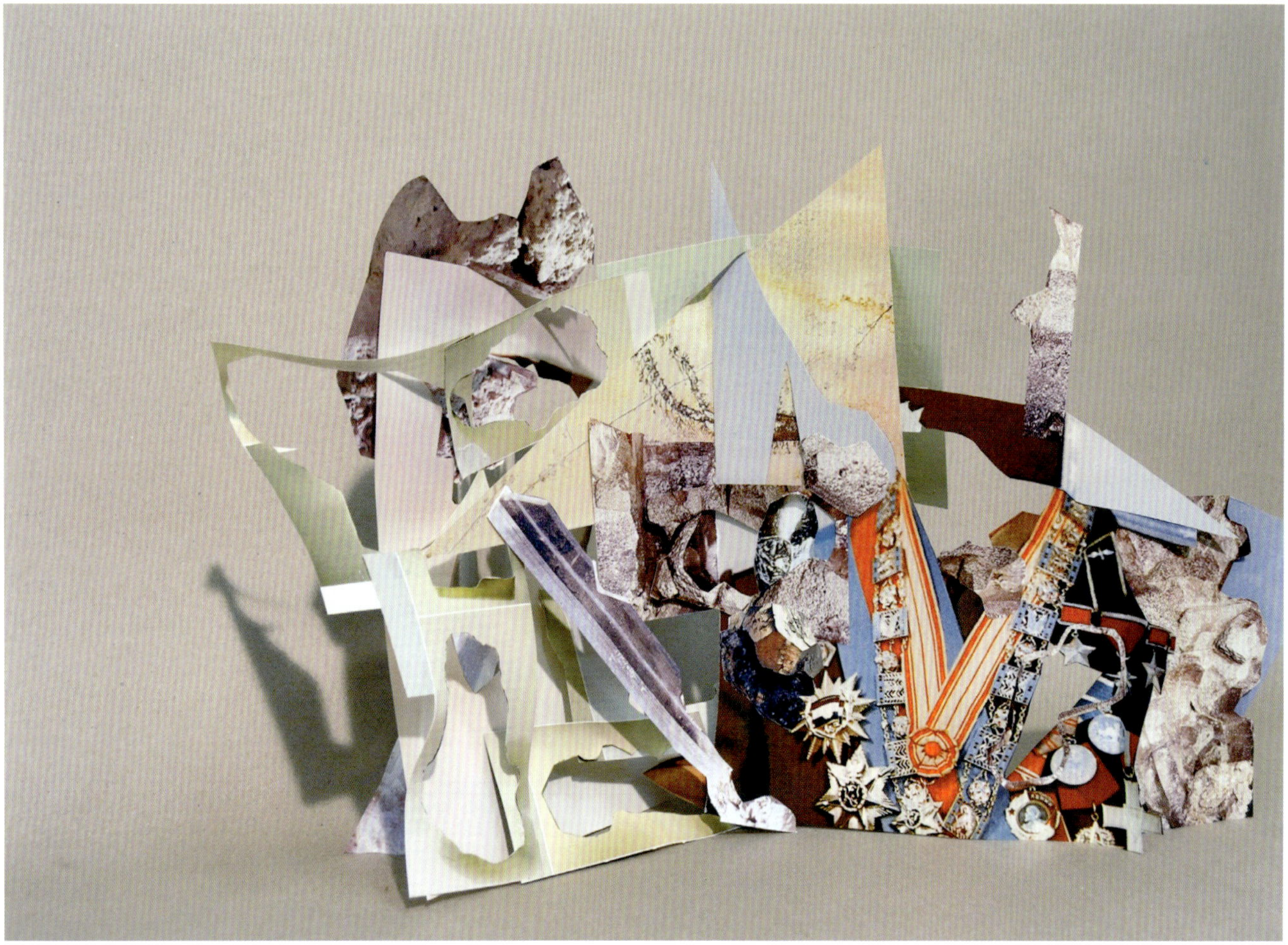

Alexis Dirks, *Medals*, 2011
16 x 11 inch digital c-print
Courtesy of the artist

Categories—their inherent violence notwithstanding—help to make sense of the world; they organize things and information into parcels that are cognitively digestible and quasi-rational. And so, what more compelling a place to initiate a discussion about interiority than with its categorical opposite: the outside?

Alexis Dirks's work is as much about the exterior as the interior. Frequently, the artist imports imagery from the outside-qua-natural world to inside the gallery space. She pairs photographic swaths of undisturbed mossy rock terrains with natural materials transformed by human intervention—a corrugated mining shelf, installed vertically to recall classical columns, and smooth pillars of mineralized core samples, mechanically extracted from the earth—things that constitute the floors and structures of built environments, which are typically categorized as distinct from the natural world. Alongside photographs of earthy floors, however, the precise cylindrical core samples evoke the pattern of birch bark rather than minerals, while the corrugated plank's knotty grain, faded and weathered, appears more tree-like than columnar. Inside the gallery space, this sleight of hand mysteriously conflates the material typologies of natural and human-built—or outside and in. In this way, Dirks reminds us that the things that comprise interiors are always imported from the outside.

What does it mean to bring the outside in? To hang an idyllic landscape in the living room or to keep potted plants on our desks? To wear bits of the earth's crust on our fingers and the residue of its physical fissions around our necks? In *Medals*, 2011, a photographed collage, Dirks invites a contemplation of material transformation; how does the raw stuff of the earth—minerals, metals and organic formations—morph into new objects, ones that are subsumed, from the outside, into our lives?

Vibrant images of raw, uncut minerals are assembled cacophonously with photos of ornamental, finely-crafted jewelry in *Medals*. Here, the artist reenacts the processes of extracting natural materials in her own process of cutting and removing images of rocks and stones from books. Hollowed pieces of paper within which the pictured rocks and stones once resided, populate the photographed assemblage; these scraps that are typically left behind stand as material evidence of the images's origin. By incorporating bits of the outsides of her chosen images, Dirks collapses the, at times deceitful, psychological and physical distance created when something is dislodged from its source, relocated and repurposed. This collapse is likewise mirrored in the simultaneous presence of images of raw resources, culled from the exterior, and their refined, sparkling, counterparts in this work.

Medals serves as a reminder to pay closer attention to the raw materials that are imported from outside, transformed and accommodated into our lives. Trees are clear cut from forests and made into furniture; gasoline is ancient decay, extracted violently from below the surface of the earth; bicycles are metal baked underground. In visually collapsing the distance between raw exterior elements and the manufactured objects around us, Dirks poetically illustrates the mutable nature of material categories. Rather than categorical opposites, the inside and out are often made of the same stuff.

Natasha Chaykowski

ARTISTS BIOS

Brea Souders was born in 1978 in Baltimore, Maryland. She currently lives and works in New York City. Souders has been exhibited in galleries and festivals internationally, including Abrons Arts Center, the Camera Club of New York and the Center for Photography at Woodstock, New York, as well as the Singapore International Photography Festival and the Peel Art Gallery, Museum and Archives. She has received a Jean and Louis Dreyfus Foundation fellowship at the Millay Colony of the Arts and a Women in Photography/LTI-Lightside Kodak materials grant.

Annie MacDonell makes photography, sculpture, film and installation. Her work questions assumptions around originality, authenticity and our constantly shifting relationship to images, both moving and still. MacDonell's work often begins with gestures of appropriation and reanimation, which spiral off into multi-layered, critical and self-reflexive meditations on the act of looking.

Aura Satz has performed, exhibited and screened her work nationally and internationally, including at the Tate Modern, Tate Britain, the Hayward Gallery, Barbican Art Gallery, ICA, the Wellcome Collection, BFI Southbank, Whitechapel Gallery, London; Oberhausen Short Film Festival, Oberhausen; the Rotterdam Film Festival, Rotterdam; the New York Film Festival, New York; Gallery 44 Centre for Contemporary Photography, Toronto; Gertrude Contemporary, Melbourne; De Appel Art Centre, Amsterdam; AV festival, Newcastle; Arnolfini, Bristol; Turner Contemporary, Margate; and BALTIC Centre for Contemporary Art, Gateshead. In 2012, she was shortlisted for the Samsung Art+ Award and the Jarman Award. She teaches at the Royal College of Art, London.

Sanaz Mazinani is a San Francisco-based visual artist, whose work explores the relationship between perception and representation. Working primarily in photography and large-scale photo-based installations, her practice intersects conceptual and formal boundaries of the photographic image in response to site, sight and insight, especially in relation to digital culture. Her work has been exhibited in the Museum Bärengasse, Zürich; Art & Architecture Library at Stanford University, Yerba Buena Center for the Arts, Asian Art Museum, San Francisco; University of Toronto Art Center; Gallery 44 Centre for Contemporary Photography, Toronto; and Emirates Financial Towers, Dubai. She has received awards and honours from the Canada Council for the Arts, San Francisco Arts Commission, Magic of Persia Contemporary Art Prize, Kala Art Institute, and the D.C. Commission on the Arts and Humanities. Her art has been written about in *Artforum*, *Flash Art*, *artnet News*, *Border Crossings*, *NOW Magazine*, *The San Francisco Chronicle*, *The Washington Post*, and *Vice*'s Creator's Project.

Sheree Hovsepian was born in Iran in 1974. She now lives in New York. Hovsepian received her BFA/BA from the University of Toledo in 1999, studied at the Glasgow School of Art, Scotland and received her MFA from the School of the Art Institute of Chicago in 2002. She has had recent solo exhibitions at Gallery 44 Centre for Contemporary Photography, Toronto; Bischoff-Weiss Gallery, London; Etemad Gallery, Dubai; and Monique Meloche Gallery, Chicago. Her work is in the permanent collections of The Studio Museum, Harlem, The Art Institute of Chicago, and the Spertus Museum, Chicago. Sheree was an artist in residence at the Banff Centre in early 2015.

Alexis Dirks is a multi-disciplinary artist currently based in Yellowknife. She graduated with an MFA from the Glasgow School of Art in 2009 and a BFA with Honours from the University of Manitoba in 2006. Exploring how the found image and object exist as raw materials for re-contextualization and the re-ordering of meaning, her work collects and re-builds these found fragments into photographs, installation and sculpture. Recent exhibitions include a solo show at TRUCK Gallery (Calgary); "Ruins", a group exhibition in the BMO Gallery, Yellowknife; "You Can't Win Them All Ladies and Gentlemen", at Library Gallery, Winnipeg; and "Yellow Font Forest Green", at Gallery 44 Centre for Contemporary Photography, Toronto.

CONTRIBUTORS BIOS

Darren Campion is a writer on photography, with occasional digressions into contemporary art and related topics. Since 2009 he has maintained *The Incoherent Light*, which is a blog dedicated to exploring various perspectives on photography. His attention is focused on expanding the discussion around the medium. He is a frequent contributor to several publications (digital and otherwise), most notably *Super Massive Black Hole*, *Of the Afternoon* and *Paper Journal*, where he has a regular series of features. Currently he is writer-in-residence at the Gallery of Photography in Dublin.

Natasha Chaykowski is a Montreal-based writer and curator. She has organized numerous exhibitions, discursive programs, and arts-based events in Toronto, Montreal, and abroad. Chaykowski held a curatorial assistant position at the Art Gallery of Ontario, co-curated the annual Emerging Artist Exhibition at InterAccess in Toronto and is the co-recipient of the 2014 Middlebrook Prize for Young Canadian Curators. She was Editorial Assistant for the *Journal of Curatorial Studies* and the Editorial Resident at *Canadian Art* Magazine in 2014. Her writing has been published in *Carbon Paper, the Art Gallery of York University, esse arts + opinions, Drain Magazine, Canadian Art,* and the *Journal of Curatorial Studies*, among other publications.

Sam Cotter is a Toronto-based artist and writer; his practice employs photography, film, installation and sculpture to focus on issues of visual representation and relationships between art and culture.

Arianne DiNardo is a writer and editor, and current Gallery Director at Propeller, an artist-run centre in Toronto. She is a founding member of Palimpsest, a curatorial and art publishing initiative, and the former Associate Editor of *OSMOS* magazine, a New-York based publication on the uses and abuses of photography.

Mark Alice Durant is an artist and writer. He has written for numerous monographs and catalogues including *Robert Heinecken: A Material History*, *McDermott and McGough: A History of Photography* and *Vik Muniz: Seeing is Believing*. He has curated several exhibitions including "Blur of the Otherworldly": "Contemporary Art, Technology and the Paranormal" and "Notes on Monumentality". He writes regularly for *Aperture* and is a contributing editor of *Dear Dave*, magazine. He is a professor in the Department of Visual Arts at the University of Maryland and faculty of the Milton Avery Graduate School for the Arts at Bard College. He is founder and editor of the online journal Saint-Lucy.com.

Peggy Gale has published extensively on time-based works by contemporary artists in numerous magazines and exhibition catalogues. She was editor of *Artists Talk 1969–1977,* from The Press of the Nova Scotia College of Art and Design, Halifax, 2004, among many other titles. A long-time independent curator, she was co-curator for "Archival Dialogues: Reading the Black Star Collection", inaugurating the Ryerson Image Centre (Toronto, 2012) and most recently, co-curator for the Biennale de Montréal 2014, titled "LÀvenir (looking forward)", at the Musée d'art contemporain de Montréal and elsewhere. In 2006, she received the Governor General's Award in Visual and Media Arts.

Ray Gilliar is a writer from Great Neck, New York. He currently lives in Brooklyn.

Sky Goodden was the founding editor of the popular contemporary art site, *BLOUIN ARTINFO Canada*, and ran its national edition from 2011 to 2014. She regularly writes for *Modern Painters, Art + Auction, Canadian Art, Border Crossings,* and *C Magazine*, among others. She was the 2010 Editorial Resident at *Canadian Art,* and holds an MFA in Criticism and Curatorial Practice from OCAD University. Goodden is the founding editor of *MOMUS* (www.momus.ca) an online international art publication that stresses a return to art criticism, launched in October 2014.

Sophie Hackett is the Associate Curator of Photography at the Art Gallery of Ontario and adjunct faculty in Ryerson University's master's program in Film and Photographic Preservation and Collections Management. She has contributed to several Canadian art magazines, international journals and monographs, and she has curated or co-curated several exhibitions and public projects at the AGO, including "Barbara Kruger: Untitled" (It), 2010; "Songs of the Future: Canadian Industrial Photographs, 1858 to Today", 2011; "Max Dean: Album, A Public Project", 2012; "Light My Fire: Some Propositions about Portraits and Photography", 2013–14; "What It Means To be Seen: Photography and Queer Visibility" and "Fan the Flames: Queer Positions in Photography", both of which opened in June 2014; and "Introducing Suzy Lake", 2014. Hackett was the lead juror for the 2014 AIMIA | AGO Photography Prize, a role she also held in 2010 and 2012.

Sara Knelman is a writer, curator and lecturer. She has taught at the Courtauld Institute of Art and Sotheby's Institute of Art, and worked as Talks Programmer at The Photographers's Gallery, London and Curator of Contemporary Art at the Art Gallery of Hamilton. She writes about photography for *Frieze* and *Source*.

Esther Leslie is Professor of Political Aesthetics at Birkbeck, University of London, UK. Her previous publications include: *Walter Benjamin: Overpowering Conformism*, 2000; a biography of Benjamin, published by Reaktion in 2007; *Hollywood Flatlands: Animation, Critical Theory, and the Avant Garde*, 2002; *Synthetic Worlds: Art, Nature and the Chemical Industry*, 2005; and *Derelicts*, a study of the effects of war on the critical writings of Benjamin, Adorno, Schwitters, Kracauer and others, 2014. She is currently writing a book on liquid crystals and together with Ben Watson runs the website militantesthetix.co.uk.

Karsten Lund is a curator and writer based in Chicago, where he has organized exhibitions at the Museum of Contemporary Art Chicago, the Museum of Contemporary Photography (MoCP), the Hyde Park Art Center, various artist-run spaces, and more unconventional sites, such as an immense factory shortly before its demolition. He recently guest curated "Phantoms in the Dirt" at MoCP, a large-scale exhibition grappling with the elemental world of matter, enigmatic traces, and photographic evidence. He has written on photography for publications such as *Art Papers, Contact Sheet,* and *Fotograf Magazine*. Lund works as a Curatorial Assistant at MCA Chicago.

Kate MacKay is the Programmer of The Images Festival as well as a visual artist, media art curator and projectionist. She is a co-founder of the screening series "Early Monthly Segments", and she has curated programs for the Innis Film Society, Cinematheque Ontario's Free Screen and Independents series. MacKay was, for many years, the primary projectionist for the Cinematheque Ontario. She has also worked as a consultant/projectionist for international film events including the Toronto International Film Festival, the Media City Film Festival, Ontario; the Flaherty Film Seminar, United States; the Markopoulos Temenos, Greece; and Harvard at the Gulbenkian, Portugal.

Caoimhe Morgan-Feir is an art writer living in Toronto. She was awarded the international Frieze Writer's Prize in 2013 and her criticism has been published in *esse arts + opinions, Journal of Curatorial Studies, Magenta, PUBLIC,* and more. She has contributed to numerous exhibition catalogues, and was the founding editor of *KAPSULA Magazine*. Most recently, she was appointed the interim online editor of *Canadian Art*.

Gabrielle Moser is a writer, educator and curator based in Toronto. She regularly contributes to Artforum.com, and her writing has appeared in venues including *Art in America, ARTnews, Fillip, Photography & Culture* and the *Journal of Visual Culture*. She has curated exhibitions for Access Gallery, Gallery TPW, Xpace and Vtape. Gabby holds a PhD in art history and visual culture from York University and teaches at OCAD University.

Kimberly Phillips is Director/Curator of Access Gallery in Vancouver, an artist-run centre committed to emergent and experimental practices. A writer and curator, Phillips holds a PhD in art history from the University of British Columbia; her studies focused on ephemeral installations in the public realm of post-1989 Berlin. Head of Interpretation at the Vancouver Art Gallery from 2009 to 2013, she regularly teaches courses in curatorial practice and visual culture at the University of British Columbia and Emily Carr University of Art + Design. She has contributed to numerous exhibition catalogues and her writings have appeared in *Artforum*, *C Magazine* and *Fillip*.

Aura Seikkula is an independent curator and researcher based in Stockholm, where she is curator for the Artipelag Konsthall. Her extensive international practice comprises of process, production and theory. Using epistemological analysis as her tool, Seikkula's current PhD research in philosophy discusses the social and cultural sustainability of artistic practices from a process perspective. Seikkula has worked in curatorial and advisory positions and curated exhibitions and events in 17 countries. She is the cofounder of SKY Finnish Society for Curators and guest curator at the Centre for Contemporary Art Lagos as well as associate curator at the Artist Pension Trust.

Sarah Robayo Sheridan is a writer and curator based in Toronto. She has worked in a variety of non-profit art organizations including art publishers, galleries, museums and festivals in Canada and internationally. She has also taught in the Department of Visual Studies at the University of Toronto at Mississauga and the Master of Visual Studies Program at the University of Toronto. She holds an MA in Curatorial Practice from the California College of the Arts. Her work as a critic and curator has received support from the Canada Council for the Arts.

Kate Steciw holds a BA from Smith College and an MFA from the School of the Art Institute of Chicago. Steciw has exhibited her art extensively in New York, most recently in group exhibitions such as: "What Is a Photograph?", the International Center of Photography; "Fixed Variable", Hauser & Wirth; "Material Images", Johannes Vogt Gallery; and "The New Romantics", Eyebeam. Recent solo exhibitions include: "Actife Plassity", Neumeister Bar-Am, Berlin; "New Custom Wall Art", Annarumma Gallery, Naples; and "Debaser", Levy Delval, Brussels. Her work has been featured in *Artforum, Art in America*, and *Interview magazine*. Steciw lives and works in Brooklyn.

Benjamin Sutton is an art critic, journalist, and curator based in Brooklyn. He is the metro editor at *Hyperallergic*, and his articles on public art, artist documentaries, the tedium of art fairs, James Franco's obsession with Cindy Sherman, and other divisive issues have appeared there and in *The L Magazine, Modern Painters, Art+Auction, BKLYNR, Artnet, Artinfo, Brooklyn Magazine*, and elsewhere. He has curated exhibitions at Field Projects, the Spring Break Art Show, the Gowanus Loft, and the Lower East Side Printshop. He studied at McGill University and the New School.

Saelan Twerdy is a freelance writer based in Montreal and a PhD candidate in Art History at McGill University. His art criticism has appeared in *Momus, Canadian Art, C magazine, Magenta, Border Crossings* and other venues.

Genevieve Yue is an assistant professor of culture and media at Eugene Lang College, The New School. She is co-editor of *Discourse: Journal for Theoretical Studies in Media and Culture* and her writing has appeared in *Grey Room, Reverse Shot, Film Comment, Film Quarterly*, and *The Times Literary Supplement*. She is currently completing a book on feminism, materiality and film theory.

Gallery 44 Centre for Contemporary Photography is a non-profit artist-run centre committed to photography as a multi-faceted and ever-changing artform. Founded in 1979 to establish a supportive environment for the development of photography, Gallery 44's mandate is to provide a context for reflection and dialogue on contemporary photography and its related practices. Gallery 44 offers exhibition and publication opportunities to national and international artists, award-winning education programmes, and affordable production facilities for artists. Through its programmes, Gallery 44 is engaged in changing conceptions of the photographic image and its modes of production.

401 Richmond Street W | Suite 120 | Toronto | Ontario
Canada M5V 3A8
Tel 416.979.3941
info@gallery44.org | www.gallery44.org
Gallery Hours: Tuesday to Saturday | 11.00 am to 5.00 pm
Registered Charity #11924 7310 RR0001

Gallery 44 would like to thank the participating artists and contributors for their support of this project.

Artists: Alexis Dirks | Sheree Hovsepian | Annie MacDonell | Sanaz Mazinani | Aura Satz | Brea Souders
Contributors: Darren Campion | Natasha Chaykowski | Sam Cotter | Arianne Di Nardo | Mark Durant | Caoimhe Morgan-Feir | Ray Gilliar | Sky Goodden | Peggy Gale | Sophie Hackett | Sara Knelman | Esther Leslie | Karsten Lund | Kate MacKay | Gabrielle Moser | Kimberly Phillips | Aura Seikkula | Sarah Robayo Sheridan | Kate Steciw | Benjamin Sutton | Saelan Twerdy | Genevieve Yue

Gallery 44 acknowledges the Publication Advisory Committee for their efforts and insights in making this project possible, thank you to: Lise Beaudry | Melissa Bennett | Jennifer Fisher | Alicia Fletcher

Thank you to Editor Lin Gibson of Lin Gibson Editorial Services, Toronto for her editorial services and support throughout this project.

G44 Centre for Contemporary Photography

Canada Council for the Arts | Conseil des arts du Canada

ONTARIO ARTS COUNCIL
CONSEIL DES ARTS DE L'ONTARIO
an Ontario government agency
un organisme du gouvernement de l'Ontario

TORONTO ARTS COUNCIL | FUNDED BY THE CITY OF TORONTO

CELEBRATING 40 YEARS

Designed by João Mota at Black Dog Publishing.

Black Dog Publishing Limited
10a Acton Street, London WC1X 9NG
United Kingdom

Tel: +44 (0)20 7713 5097
Fax: +44 (0)20 7713 8682
info@blackdogonline.com
www.blackdogonline.com

British Library Cataloguing-in-Publication Data. A CIP record for this book is available from the British Library.

ISBN 9781910433027

Black Dog Publishing Limited, London, UK, is an environmentally responsible company. *Reflections Refractions* is printed on sustainably sourced paper.

cover image
Aura Satz, *Doorway for Natalie Kalmus* (still), 2013

reuse recycle reduce

art design fashion
history photography
theory and things

black dog publishing
london uk

www.blackdogonline.com